NOV 9 2006

Love and love each
precious day.
Tricia
10.3.03

Maltese Crossing:
Love, Loss, and Lessons of Compassion

By Kuan Yin

May 1993 — March 1997
As told to Dr. P. D. Sargent

Illustrations by Marie Cole

Golden Reflections Publications
Golden, Colorado

Maltese Crossing: Love, Loss, and Lessons of Compassion

© Copyright 2002 by P.D. Sargent.
All rights reserved
Printed by Sunrise Design and Printing Company
Delon and Paul Chau
Printed in China

No part of this book may be used or reproduced in any manner whatsoever without written permission from the publishers except in the case of brief quotations embodied in critical articles and reviews.

First Edition
First Printing

Graphic Design by Karen Saunders, Denver, CO
Illustrations by Marie Cole, Littleton, CO
Edited by Barbara McNichol, Tucson, AZ

Library of Congress Cataloging-in-Publication Data
Sargent, Patricia D.
 Maltese Crossing: Love, Loss, and Lessons of Compassion
Sargent. –1st edition
p. 156

ISBN 0-9720022-0-0
PCN Library of Congress Number: pdh32868

Sargent, Patricia D, 1935-
1. Pets   2. Grief   3. Self-Help
I. Title

Published by
Golden Reflections Publications
Golden, Colorado

Table of Contents

Table of Illustrations vii

Introduction ix

Acknowledgments xi

Dedication xii

Special Thank You xv

A Heavenly Happening 1

The Turkish Bath 9

What's in a Name? 15

Family Planning 25

Wardrobe for Saints, Goddesses, and Toxic Talismans 33

Travel is Travail 41

Please Don't Even Mention It 49

People and Parties: Silver Slippers and Combat Boots 55

Nothing Seems to Fit 63

Kuan Yin's Commandments to Mistresses 69

The Final Analysis 77

Wind, Harbinger of Change 85

Tail of the Tale 99

Good Grief 109

Journey of the Red Balloon 117

Posthumous Tribute 123

Resources 127

Table of Illustrations

Chapter Title	Illustration Title	Page Number
Acknowledgments	*Friends Indeed*	xiii
A Heavenly Happening	*Incarnation Nouveau*	7
The Turkish Bath	*The Turkish Bath*	11
What's in a Name?	*Dual Deities*	19
Family Planning	*Elizabethan Ruff*	29
Wardrobes	*The Wind and the Rain*	37
Travel is Travail	*The Treasure Box*	43
Please, Don't Even Mention It	*The Sentinel*	51
People and Parties	*Dinner Party Dangers*	61
The Final Analysis	*The Nightmare*	79
The Final Analysis	*The Transition*	83
Wind, the Harbinger of Change	*The Birthday Party*	95
Tail of the Tale	*In the Driver's Seat*	107
Journey of the Red Balloon	*The Red Balloon*	121

Friends Indeed

Thanks to all my human and animal companions. Blessings enough to go all around.

Special Thank You

Many thanks to friends who read and commented on the manuscript. I especially want to thank Melanie Mulhall and Donniece Sage, who gave in-depth reactions to the work. Thanks, too, to Barbara Wagner, Lissa Forbes Knoche, Linda Carlson, Michelle Carlson, Jimmy Riley, and Daniel Raphael who helped with renaming the manuscript when the tone change came with the loss of Kuan Yin. Thanks to my friends, Arline Rustin, Dr. Judith Girard, and Doris Anderson who were great cheerleaders and kept cheering especially when I fell into the sorrowful times.

When I lost Kuan Yin, Colorado State University was gracious in allowing me to use the resource information gleaned from their research. I send them my heartfelt thanks for their generosity. They kindly permitted me to publish web site numbers, hot lines, and other public information included in the Resources chapter. Research data, including "Suggested Reading," is rephrased from documents included in a packet they send to grieving clients in their community. I have commented on my experiences as described in their research. I have also updated the list of resources and titles to include recent publications since 1998.

Most grateful thanks to Marie Cole of Fruit of the Spirit, the artist whose precious paintings have captured the essence of Kuan Yin. Thanks and double thanks to my editor Barbara McNichol of Barbara McNichol Editorial, graphic designer Karen Saunders of MacGraphics Services, desktop publishing consultant Bill Steffensmeier of Copy Max, research specialist Barbara Wagner of The Access Point, web site designer Ken Dubrovin, and printers Delon and Paul Chau of Sunrise Design and Printing, China. Most grateful thanks to Colorado Independent Publishers Association, and tender thanks to my patient husband, Dick Sargent.

P.D. Sargent, MM, 2002

A Heavenly Happening

Yes, I am Kuan Yin. People say I am an adorable Maltese puppy dog, but *dog* is not what I think of myself. Nor do I know one who would refer to me as "a dog." I have chosen the body of a Maltese puppy to serve special souls who need extraordinary care and comfort from a Bodhisattva. As you may know, Bodhisattva is a Buddhist term for a very spiritual being. Bodhisattvas have attained *prajna*—the state of pure knowledge—in their own earthly incarnation. I have postponed Nirvana to help others on their own journey to attain enlightenment. Nirvana is what you might call Paradise, the condition of salvation and peace. It is, in fact, freedom from eternal reincarnations that cause suffering. I have come to help a woman who is retired, single, and very much alone. The Gods have sent me to show her that professional life is not real life. She, like many others, thinks that what one does is who one is. Not true.

My name is not simply regal; it is heavenly. Kuan Yin, as you know, is the Far Eastern Goddess of Mercy. The most powerful deity in the Chinese pantheon, in that incarnation, I had also been the most popular deity before the revolution in China. For centuries, I have been honored in every Buddhist home as the symbol of human compassion. Ironically, my Mistress researched names for weeks before my arrival at her home in Denver. She obviously thought her life *needed* mercy; else why would she need a goddess to reign over her home? Although she knew that Kuan Yin is recognized as a goddess who teaches through comfort and mercy, my Mistress thought she was only choosing a puppy, when in fact she chose the salvation of her soul.

I did, indeed, come from the East. One might concede the kennel in Nebraska *is* Far East from the condominium in Denver. For three long hours, I traveled *en caravan* from Lexington, Nebraska, to Julesburg, Colorado, and three more long hours traveling from Julesburg to my new home in Denver. For the first leg of my journey, my traveling companion was a miniature French poodle who had been my Lady in Waiting, so to speak, since my last littermate had sojourned to far-off lands to meet her new human companion. I spent the second leg of my journey bonding with my new Mistress, to gain her trust, and to train her how to hold me without squishing my tiny insides. I was, at that time, only three-and-a-half pounds.

You are undoubtedly aware that people think *they* own their animal companions. Popular folk wisdom says one may own a dog, but a *cat owns* the owner. Perhaps that is true for the *common* run of dogs, but the *Maltese* is more like the cat—we also own our human companions. We do not *advertise* the fact that we rule; we *know* we rule but we like to make our humans think *they* do. Unlike cats, however, Maltese do not act superciliously or surreptitiously. We do not hold ourselves apart, acting smugly until dinnertime.

It is simply a matter of finesse. Like every wife who knows the subtleties of training a new husband, we wisely make the decisions that affect the quality of partnered life, yet we allow our humans to think they thought of the ideas themselves. It gives one great satisfaction and allows one's humans to feel they are in control. An educator by profession, my Mistress is, after all, a Master Control-Taker.

The Maltese is the Empress of dogs and the Companion of royalty. We deserve to be addressed respectfully. Once my Mistress and I went to visit my sister Cecilia at her owner's penthouse. My Mistress called me a "nice little doggie" when she thought I did something rather pleasing. I had hardly noticed the tag when Cecilia's human companion, Dr. Anderson, corrected her immediately. "No, no, my dear, not *doggie*. You must say, 'nice *little girl.*'" CeCe had trained her human well.

Dr. Anderson sounded indignant, to say the least, and I appreciated her intercession. When one is training a new mistress, one relies on all training resources available. Owners of my Breed of Champions are the greatest resources. They have seen our "papers," which show we are descended from a long line of supreme champions, blue-ribboned winners, and jeweled be-dazzlers of blue-blooded princesses, queens, and empresses from all realms—even from the most ancient of times. Empresses and queens of the mightiest empires have loved their tiny canine companions. Some have even taken them with them to the very ends of their lives.

For example, when the French Queen Marie Antoinette was beheaded in 1793, her powdered coiffeur—symbol of the hated *ancien régime*—dropped with her head into the waiting basket below the scaffold. As the guillotine fell, a tiny white dog scampered from under the many crinolines of her skirts. Surely that was a Maltese, the gift for Empresses. One might wonder how the little dog stayed so quiet during all the shouting of the rabble and that dreadful crowd. Any symbol of beauty or luxury—which the Maltese surely is—was in great danger I fear. Like Marie Antoinette, Dr. Anderson and other Maltese Mistresses hold their loyal companions closely and treat them like the treasures from heaven that they are.

There has always been the allure of the roar of the crowd. Back in the earliest of days, mankind roared in tribal clusters as they went in for the kill of bison, mastodon, or wildebeest. In Roman times, crowds gathered in large clusters in a coliseum to watch the killing of their own kind. I have read about modern versions of coliseum activity, and although humans no longer actually put their opponents to the sword, the crowd still screeches, "Kill, Kill!" Through the years—in revolutions, Olympic games, on New Year's Eve, and even in Fourth of July Parades—people still like to make noise. What do you suppose it means when people surround themselves with so much noise? Are they making a show of power? Does the noise of a crowd give people courage? Do people just enjoy the sounds of their own vocal chords?

Humans are noisy, you know. Even two thousand years after the Roman Empire, humans create noises …*en mass* and alone. They invent machines that make noise when they can't get a crowd together to make noise with them. They have household machinery like the furnace and the refrigerator that turn themselves on and off with a whoosh or a hum or a very unnerving click. They have ceiling fans that whir and obscene equipment like hair dryers and vacuum cleaners that whine and roar. People play the radio and listen to endless music and crass voices all the day long. Sometimes they play the television, which further stimulates their senses by adding a *visual image* of the speaker.

When I have had enough of noise, I prance to the bedroom and my *boudoir*. *Boudoir* means a soft bed with a snuggly blanket in which to bury oneself when the noise of humans rankles one's serenity. At least there, I do not have to listen to the repetition of violence, abuse, and neglect that so fascinates humans. I can content myself with slumbering, cogitating, or meditating. In the comfort of my carefully arranged cushions, I can even plan a stratagem for the future training of my Mistress. That is unless, on rare occasion, the bedroom television happens to be on. My Mistress likes the news.

The news in particular puzzles me. Watching newscasters is like viewing most newspaper photographs: BOPSA, the view is called. Have you ever seen photos in the papers showing a Bunch of People Standing Around (or sitting, as the case may be)? Why do newscasters smile while their partners report yet another terrible story? They patiently wait their turn to reveal an even more terrible event with decorum and a sense of finesse. The news program is like a card game with reporters waiting to slap down their winning card or—in this case—shocking statement. I wonder why they grin widely into the camera to show their white teeth. Some also pull their mustachioed lips up to display both tooth and gum. Why do they smile at each other at even the most heinous announcements, and congratulate each other often? If a puppy showed *his* teeth so frequently, his human would scold the poor thing!

Let me digress a moment to give you a canine view of finesse. Take potty training, for example. My Mistress brooded before my arrival that her Oriental carpets would soon be in great danger. So she cordoned off a small area of hallway tile, placing my bed at one end and newspapers *all over* the other end of the floor. Somewhere in the middle of the hallway, she placed the food and water because she had read in many books that Maltese, like any civilized creature, do not foul their eating and sleeping areas. Even at the age of seven months, I want to assure you, Maltese *know* the difference between *boudoir* and *bidet*! We are discerning and discriminating.

Of course, my Mistress feared if she did not put down enough papers, "accidents" would happen, so she put down newspapers *everywhere*. I have seen so many newspapers that I have now begun to read. I notice she always puts the sports pages on the floor. Sports pages are fine, but I prefer the financial pages myself. Obviously, my Mistress feels they are less expendable than the sports pages though, for there is a plethora of the latter all over the floor. She once confided she thought the original intention of printing that section was to line the bottom of birdcages. I did not grasp her gist, but I quickly got sick of the slick advertisement center pages because the colored print got all over my beautiful, silken-haired paws.

The newsprint also turned my delicate feet dingy. My skirts were gray instead of the lustrous white for which I am so well known. The hated newsprint, fortunately, did not discolor my tail for, as you know, I carry that proudly above me. It's curled as tight as a corkscrew to let my fine plumage arrange itself like a flag unfurled, streaming along as I scamper from one end of the hall to the other.

Incarnation Nouveau

*My name is not simply regal; it is heavenly. Kuan Yin,
as you know, is the Far Eastern Goddess of Mercy.*

At the end of the first week, my Mistress was as disgruntled as I was with newspapers everywhere. She saw that I was mostly gray from muzzle to hock. We found newsprint on the bottom of her shoes, ink all over my silken skirts, and a fine imprint of the football scores on the tile in front of her bedroom door. I took pity on her and decided enough was enough.

Remember, I am Kuan Yin, respected Goddess. I had consistently used the same spot, approximately, to deposit my gift to the sports world, to show her that her animal companion could be trusted to aim carefully, to assure her the carpets would be safe. As a result of my keen sensibility, she removed the newspapers from the far end of the room—as if she thought *she* was training *me*. I suppose she felt satisfied because that outcome was predicted in the official dog book. Nevertheless, I cannot tell you how sick *I* was of disheveled newspapers spread all over my living quarters!

The Turkish Bath

Besides, as my appearance became grayer, my Mistress's facial expression became one of distress. MM, for that is what I now call her, began to slump—to walk less proud—to hang her head in shame. Cleanliness was part of her daily *mantra*, and I, her personal companion and dearest friend, was not clean. I was, in fact, a mess! When I looked in the mirror, I did not recognize myself. I looked like I had been rolling in newsprint, for behold, that is exactly what I had been doing. MM's darling, dainty, and delicate Maltese looked ever more like a canine rag lady. MM's skin became sallow. Her jowls grew longer, her eyes drooped, and she simply did not look like a mistress I could take out in public. She grumbled more frequently, and then she did an absolutely terrible thing. She gave me a *bath.*

She gave no warning. I was cozying up in her lap (my breed excels in adorable lap-warming) when she carried me quietly to the sink surrounded by bottles of tearless shampoo, scented conditioner, combs, brushes, towels, and a hair dryer. She filled the bottom of the sink with a little water and lowered me, ankle-deep, into Basic H™, a substance certain to loosen the gritty black ink from my nails and paws. Horrors! What deception! Then, just as I got used to the warm wetness, she started to slosh the water from a waterfall onto to my back, my legs, and my distinguished tail. What a shock to my system! I trembled, more from dread than cold. The water was warm enough, but I couldn't trust this woman to cease this ordeal by water. What would be next?

Next, of course, she immersed my head, my ears, and my tear-stained face. She shampooed me gently, lathering me carefully so she wouldn't mat or tangle my hair. I heard her giggling as she commented that, wet, I looked like a white rat. Well, if Cecelia's owner, Dr. Anderson, were insulted with my being called a *dog*, what would she think of my being called a *rat*? It would be quite a while before I would forgive this woman for this new indignity.

Then MM cooed at me and called me a "good girl." She rinsed and dried me until I thought my tender skin would absorb the endless small towels in which she swaddled me to absorb the water. I looked at her pitifully and made a soul connection. My gaze coaxed her to hug me closely. She obediently complied. Eye contact is powerful. Even goldfish know about the Power of the Gaze. Patient and long-suffering creatures, their motto, like that of politicians, is, "for food or applause, just rise to the top and make eye contact on the way." With eye control, I certainly had *her Nibs* trained. I must remember *that very look* for future reference. I was proud that my training abilities were increasing—now that I had her removing extraneous papers (well, at least the slick advertising sections). And I even had her hugging me and *apologizing* for getting me all wet.

The Turkish Bath

*My gaze coaxed her to hug me closely. Eye contact is powerful.
Even goldfish know about the Power of the Gaze.*

I didn't stay wet for long, however, as she continued to blot me dry and take me into the bathroom to use the turbo-engined wind machine on my tiny body. The roar of the machine overwhelmed me. I did not know if fire would follow the stream of hot air that swooshed over my bare, shivering body. I wanted to hide under my blanket to remove myself as far as possible from the tumultuousness of the dryer. I couldn't bear the din. No matter where I moved, the insistent stream of hot air followed me. My Mistress, like Gulliver in the land of the little people, had only to hold on to my rib cage to inhibit my movement. Being a featherweight, I was no match for her strength, her energy, or her determination. Ah, but wit and wisdom will win out. I wiggled and gave her *that imploring look ...* and for an instant she loosened her grip. I was at last free to run from corner to corner of the tiled powder room to avoid the jet stream, but the hot monsoon winds, aimed at my tender underpinnings, followed me.

No part of me—breech, brisket, chest, nor croup—was sacred. As I was drying out, my silken hair returned and fluffed out like virgin goose down. The feathered fringe around my paws flared over my pink nails.

At last the machine grew quiet and my Mistress again cooed, "Good girl." Little did she know how good I *really* was. If I were not named after that Goddess of Mercy, I would have bitten that dryer in half! I would have torn that grooming brush bristle from bristle! And I would have shredded those flimsy towels! Well, at least I would have barked.

To train my Mistress not to wash me again, I carefully aimed at the same, one-and-only newspaper. As I predicted, she eliminated more of the athletic ground cover. I had only to tolerate one neatly placed sports page at a time. If I walked carefully, instead of rolling over enthusiastically on the paper, I could keep my silken sheen, and she would know I certainly did not need another bath. I walked straight and tall. I barked when I wanted her to remove the soiled sports page, and I stood smiling as she took satisfaction in what she thought was *her* own job well done. She was going to be easier to train than I had imagined.

It would be only a matter of days when I would loll luxuriously on the Oriental carpets, a privilege I so richly deserved. Had my breed not reclined on a Sultana's footstool or the Odalisques prayer rug? For one whose ancestors had enjoyed the run of the Seraglio, what were these Chinese carpets to me? For the moment, however, I curled up in my *boudoir*, a deep foam-rubber chiropractic pillow covered with a monogrammed woolen throw. My Mistress loved me so much, she gave up her monogrammed lap robe so I would be warm. What a good girl!

What's In a Name

I am confused. My Mistress seems to have many names. At work, her colleagues call her Pat, her close friends call her Tricia, her students call her Doc, and her mail reads Dr. P. D. Campbell. Personally I think she has watched the television mystery "Rumpole of the Old Bailey" so much that she identifies with Rumpole's wife, whom he secretly calls, "She Who Must Be Obeyed." No matter what my Mistress is called, she knows in her heart it is really the latter.

In her mind, there are really only two ways to do things: the wrong way and *her* way. I have had to work hard to show her there are three ways, including *my* way. When I was waiting to come to the Campbell Museum—so called because of the mountains of books and other collections—the breeder tried to acquaint me with people-living, dealing with humans' noises and their strange ways. When my last littermate left the kennel, I moved into the breeder's farmhouse where it was warm, cozy, and, well, casual. The breeder watched me carefully for signs of my physical needs and took me outdoors to relieve myself. I scarcely had time to train her to use newspapers indoors (so I did not have to subject myself to the cold outdoors) before a long-distance telephone call came. On that call, Dr. Campbell agreed to meet the breeder half way from my kennel to her condominium. She was going to adopt me!

I had no idea what kind of woman this doctor was, but I wasn't about to spend all my life getting shots from some needle-happy veterinarian. Turns out she was not "that kind" of doctor. She was simply a school administrator: a high school principal and a sometimes college professor. What a relief! For lack of something better to call me, the breeder started calling me "Katie." "K, K, K, Katie," sang her husband, the farmer. How revolting. I was hoping this "doctor" would think of something much more dignified. Can you imagine canine fans crowding around to say insipid things like, "Kiss me, Kate." Fortunately, I had little need to train my new Mistress on the issue of names, for she had already picked one, which, I assure you, I had planted in her mind long before she chose the name. I soon answered to my own name, Kuan Yin, which was much more distinguished and far more appropriate than the dreadful "Katie." It was also my destiny.

Kuan Yin, as I said before, is the revered Chinese Goddess of Mercy. "That's a funny name," I mused. I thought my breed sprang from Arab origins; my Mistress told me that Malta was once peopled with Arabs. How Arabs found their way to that little island off the southern coast of Sicily is more than I can fathom. Maybe they carried their little white dogs with them across the desert to this island landing spot on their way to conquer Spain and other parts of the Western world. Traveling in a caravan on the Silk Road, maybe the little white dog foraged through wind-blown and sand-beaten human skin to relieve its humans of fleas. No, on second thought, I am sure Maltese dogs were bred to be people pleasers. My birth mother told me so. Those Arabs must have brought my tiny, silken ancestors from their homeland to give as gifts to Persian potentates. They would certainly add to the luxury of Sultan's favorites and King's wives, or to mighty dowagers whose money could finance the conquerors' holy wars. Maybe the little white dogs licked the wounds of the travelers on their way to conquest, or just comforted them by kissing their faces to tell them they were glad to have them home for a bit. Some rumors say Maltese dogs did not really originate in the Mediterranean at all. Perhaps, it is said, they came from Asia or even Egypt. Maltese is a very old breed.

Well, you know, Egyptians loved their cats. They loved them so much that, when their pets died, they had them embalmed. They buried their beloved cats in huge cemeteries in Egypt—cemeteries made just for cats. My Mistress has told me that when archaeologists started exploring the pyramids, exhuming the mummies, and shipping the treasure to their own hometowns, they also sent cat-mulched soil back to enrich English gardens. Now, that's not what *I* read, mind you; that's what my Mistress *told me*. I only read the sports page, you know.

Ancient Egyptians had a mysterious dog in their pantheon of gods. The face of Anubis, the god of the Dead, they say, is not like any dog identified today. If you want to know what I think, however, I think Anubis looked just like the toy Manchesters I have met. Yes they do. Toy Manchesters have large beady eyes, erect and alert "mule" ears, skinny bodies, long legs, and delicate long-nailed paws. And they are black—just like Anubis. Hmm, if little black dogs lived in Egypt, I'll bet little white dogs lived there, too. Well, as I said, I only know what I read in the newspapers. Unfortunately, dog shows and historical data rarely make headlines in the sports section.

My Mistress reads voraciously about the ancient world. She corrected my original impressions of an Arab heritage and told me that my breed may, indeed, have originated in the mystical world of ancient Egypt. Inscriptions and frescoes on tomb walls in early dynastic Egypt have pictured dogs other than the mystical and magical lord of the dead. She said the paintings depicted four breeds of dogs reflecting the canine population in 3500 BCE. Breeds recognizable today include the mastiffs and Maltese. MM says the Phoenicians—the great seafarers of the Mediterranean—may well have traded their purple dye for white dogs in Egypt, traded these white dogs to the people of Malta for olive oil and textiles, then traded white dogs, textiles, and olive oil to their descendants in Carthage in North Africa. The Carthaginians held a monopoly of maritime trade in the ancient world. The Egyptians, it seems, loved only the waters of their sacred Nile River. They would, MM has said, leave the dangerous sea voyages to the mercantile investors in their mother country Phoenicia. That country, she believes, was a dangerous place for infants, small animals, and snails, which produced the precious purple dye. MM told me that the Murex is a snail found on the coast of Lebanon, or ancient Phoenicia, and Carthage in North Africa, which was founded by the Phoenicians. Snails were crushed by the ton to produce a beautiful purple dye, which the nobility of all the lands around the Mediterranean used. So costly was the dye that only monarchs and the wealthiest of people could afford to wear the color purple.

Dual Deities

Hmm, if little black dogs lived in Egypt's pantheon, I'll bet little white dogs lived there too.
We are God of the Dead, and Goddess of Life.

The Carthaginians, like their ancestors the Phoenicians, worshipped the goddess Tanit and her consort Baal. When winds didn't blow in the right direction, when the crops didn't grow, when plagues or pestilences swept the land, or *any fool thing* went awry, the people sacrificed their tiny children to appease the gods. When the people rose up in protest, the Carthaginians soon substituted innocent animals in place of their own babies on the sacrificial altar. My Mistress told me the Greek king Agamemnon thought nothing of appeasing the Thracian winds by lashing his own daughter Iphigenia to the masts and slaying her to appease the goddess Artemis.

For that matter, the Hebrew patriarch Abraham willingly bound his only son Isaac on a sacrificial stone altar because his god wanted to test his love. People and animals have suffered greatly because of myth or tribal beliefs. When human sacrifice ceased, people sacrificed animals like sheep, ewe lambs, rams, oxen, young heifers, bulls, and pigs. Heaven only knows that some people, right into the twenty-first century, actually stuffed starving live dogs with rice, killed them, then roasted them on a spit to fill their own bellies. So be careful when you shrug and say, "It's a dog's life!"

With luck, the Egyptian god Anubis, who greets the dead, found no little white dogs as substitute sacrifices to the gods on Egyptian altars. The keeper of the tombs of Egypt weighed the heart of the dead against the weight of a feather. The heart of a Maltese, of course, is mighty. The dog fears nothing, and I would imagine the sheer weight of my heart would exceed all the feathers of the ibis, the vulture, and the hawk—in fact, all the sacred birds of the great Nile. On thinking it over, it would be wise to note the Egyptians probably meant "guilt" when they talked about weight of the heart. The Maltese is the great comforter; its pure heart bears no guilt, for it is made of gilt, pure gold. On second thought, our hearts, though mighty, must be lighter than a feather.

Anubis, with his magic, narrow eyes like the Doberman, may have evolved into the toy Manchester and, through deliberate breeding, may have developed rich, round, deep black eyes like mine. And while Anubis represented the underworld, his descendants represent the less serious quality of earthly terrain. Forgotten today is the solemnity and gravity of preparing for death. I never find that subject on the sports page, anyway.

After all, humans are busy taking care of the here and now. They do not have time, as the ancient Egyptians did, to prepare for the hereafter. Some, I have heard, give no thought to the concept. Some don't even take good care of the present.

In the here and now, my distinguished breed celebrates life and the human condition with joy and oftimes a little levity. Alas, as we all know, the human condition is filled with universal pains and woes that humans bring upon themselves: traumatic stresses of the marketplace, unwise selection of lovers, scars from the battle between avarice and altruism, and, sometimes, a dose of melancholia.

From the human condition—strife, worry, and fear of death—we lap dogs have learned our greatest secrets. From the years of couching our tiny beings on the laps of wealth, power, and leadership, we have learned the deep secrets of human hearts. From their pain, we have gathered the wisdom of the universe. We have also developed the great art of listening. If humans were to learn more about the universal heart and train themselves to listen better, they would not need our services. That would mean, of course, we would be out of a job. We come into their lives to help humans develop their souls, to raise soul standards, so to speak. Troubled humans need patience and comfort—just the virtues for which Maltese are valued. Because we have stored this knowledge in our genes—just like Dachshunds were trained to be ratters and Labradors were bred to be retrievers—we Maltese have come to be known as comforters. We simply look and listen, absorb the pain, and reflect the joy. Even humans could do that if they so desired.

Perhaps, like humans who have named their children after the precious virtues Faith, Hope, and Charity, we Maltese should be called Comfort. Some humans have even named themselves after gemstones like Pearl, Opal, Ruby, and Sapphire. With such levity, the Romans, after giving up the Great Mother goddess, appeased women by affixing their names to great virtues like Constanzia, Roma, Nike, and Victory. However, they honored those virtues, as they did their women, by completely ignoring them and acting in most unvirtuous manners at Entertainments and Tributes. Actually, by naming their women after virtues and placing the ideal woman on an unreachable pedestal, Romans essentially obviated woman's real value as humans. MM wonders what those women thought about the "Newspeak" in Rome and other places in their Brave New World Empire. Surely Roman women recognized the contradiction of the appearance of reverence and the reality of suppression. Women, who could not vote and were not considered citizens, accepted the social graces instead of enjoying full participation in society. Alas, they don't write about that in the sports page, either.

As for my name, I am grateful. I am glad to have been named after the Goddess of Mercy, for I know how to handle mercy, gentleness, and comfort. It really doesn't matter, however, since my Mistress often confuses me by calling me by many other names such as "Sweetie," "Puddies," and "Precious." I believe those names are synonyms for Comfort, so I am satisfied.

Unfortunately, not all animals are so appreciated. In the Doggie Discipline Class, I even trained with a beagle whose human "companion" attached to him the nickname Dammit.

"Dammit," the master would say, "get over here." The master thought he was cute. MM thinks he is probably the same man who makes his dog ride in the back of a truck bed with no side rails.

Family Planning

No one thinks of hospitals as being places of worship, but certainly much praying takes place there. My Mistress has prayed for me many times. At each stage of my progression from my puppyhood through adulthood, she has worried about my health and well-being. Just as she worried over her children's illnesses, she fears losing me. She never guesses the real reason for my being with her. Humans are only aware of the moment. They do not examine the underlying reason for change, which must inevitably come if they are to develop into something better—to achieve a higher plane.

I was no more than six months old when she took me to the animal hospital to have me spayed. At that phase of my incarnation, I did not realize how unseemly motherhood would be to a Goddess of Mercy; however, it is true that mothers are really *earthly forms* of The Goddess. By their very natures, mothers must also practice mercy and comforting—not only to their own progeny, but also to those of their neighbors. Nonetheless, it is a modern tradition to limit the fertility of earth creatures, at least those with four legs. The concept is catching on with humans, but they seem to limit it only to those who would *best* benefit society by having more children. Motherhood was not in the picture for me, for I needed to mother my Mistress.

I had a fair inkling that progeny might be an annoyance, or perhaps only a hindrance, for the work of a Bodhisattva so I accepted the fate of this incarnation and allowed my tiny body to surrender the accoutrements of parenthood. MM, of course, cried when she handed my pet taxi over to the vet's assistant. I thought it strange that, while *I* had to experience the anesthesia, the incision, and the recovery, *she also* felt the pain. I realized at once that my human felt intense, if vicarious, psychic pain. And as she felt my pain, I assumed a little of hers. The pain drew us closer together. Pain and adversity often connect people. That, in celestial circles, is called empathy.

The surgery took place at the veterinary services section of a large pet supply facility. PetsMart™ was a one-stop shop to provide for my care. There, I had undergone my first body probes when MM took me for the initial "puppy" check and the battery of immunization injections that would keep me healthy. There, too, we shopped for puppy food, combs and brushes, and other special needs. MM bravely yet gently held me for the doctor's prods and pricks with the magic serums that would protect my earthly body from strange diseases. Introducing me to the world of germs and microbes, she felt she was acting responsibly to protect me, so I forgave her. She said she loved me and wanted to keep me around for a *very* long time. She had set her heart on the prognosis of the veterinarian that Maltese can live to enjoy a fifteen-year life span.

My Mistress hadn't had a dog in her home in more than three decades. In fact, although her family collected a couple of mongrels and a black Labrador retriever over the years, she had never had her own loving animal companion. Her sons had always chosen animals they could wrestle, pals who would leap across streams, chase birds and bullfrogs, and play Frisbee with them. MM had never known the companionship and loyalty that only certain breeds could satisfy for her. When she retired from a demanding career as a high school principal, she mostly needed peace, appreciation, and affection—things a job cannot provide. Her entire life had been spent caring for others: her own three children, hundreds of students at the school, and her dying mother. All had needed medical attention and, at times, traumatic intervention.

The purpose of my reincarnation was to teach and administer mercy, patience, and compassion. Bodhisattvas remain in the lives of our special humans until they understand the true quality of mercy and its relationship to unconditional love. We choose how long our special humans need us and help them to untangle the pain of their lives that they themselves have caused. As MM could never understand celestial signals, I used my "adorable look" to assure her I could manage the discomfort and indignities required of this mission. She tended to me as she would her own baby, and I tended to her as her personal loving spirit.

My recuperation was progressive. I could not, however, tolerate the big white sock MM had tied around my tiny middle to keep me from removing my stitches before the incision had properly healed. MM explained that if I succeeded in rubbing off the sock as I rubbed up against the wall, the sofa, or the chaise lounge, she would have to let the professionals put an Elizabethan collar around my neck to keep the itchy incision intact. I thought of Sir Walter Raleigh, Ann Boleyn, and Mary Queen of the Scots and wondered about all the ruffs supporting the necks of the English queen and those in her court. I wondered if they also had stitches bothering them somewhere. My curiosity aside, MM checked the incision each day, and each time I loosened the sock, she made it snug once again. MM is a very determined human.

Soon, I was up and around learning new skills to please her and to teach her, through eye contact, how to read my thoughts and provide for my earthly needs. Somehow we got through the ordeal. An eager learner, she responded to my reward system to reinforce her training. Whenever she met my needs, I gave her a little kiss on the hand, a loving gaze, or an attitude of appreciation. These she obviously needed as part of the service I was sent to give her.

As the years passed, we grew closer and MM grew ever more solicitous. She was my constant companion, and I was hers. When I peered over the edge of the bathtub, curiously watching how carefully she washed her face, she offered to wash my "facie" too. When she did, I knew we were going to visit someone or entertain a special visitor. Although it was an effort for me, I allowed her to primp and preen my face, my bows, and my luxurious white hair to her heart's content. Always gentle, she spent many evenings brushing my silken tresses. In these hours, she did not focus on insignificant pursuits such as goals, achievements, and success. No worrisome thoughts broke into the quiet moments of my grooming. MM concentrated on long, smooth strokes of the brush to groom my glowing white hair. She hummed softly as she brushed and spoke loving words that

The Elizabethan Ruff

*I wondered . . . with all the ruffs supporting the necks of English royalty . . .
if they had stitches bothering them somewhere too.*

made me feel I had her complete attention. I was, indeed, her work of art, her constant companion, her confidante, and friend.

I was also her link to other humans. When we needed Eukanuba™ for my supper, we traveled to the supermarket to collect our staples. MM had to leave the enclosure of her house to take me to the groomer, to purchase our food, to take me to the veterinarian's office. When she took me for a walk on the lead, she practiced the things we learned in the discipline class. MM was indeed getting out more, seeing more people, and talking to everyone. Strangers who also thought I was adorable would stop her in the market to chat about their own treasured companion animals—even those now long gone. MM talked about me, of course, but she also inquired about their dog or cat. She began to understand how important animals are to humans, and she empathized with people who had lost them.

She took me almost everywhere. When we went to the beauty salon, I sat patiently and safely in my pet taxi as I watched her endure the bleaching, washing, and blow-drying I so abjured when I went to the groomer. Fortunately, she did not allow the groomer to cover my luminous white fur with color nor bleach the stains on my face, as show dogs must endure. But she seemed to think that yellow hair, at least for her, was more stylish than white or gray. There was something ironic that I, a purebred Maltese who could be a show dog, was lovingly kept as a well-tended companion. On the other hand, she, who could now slip softly into a comfortable stage of life, endured the very procedures she would not allow me to suffer.

Perhaps I had a "show human" on my hands. But I don't understand. If white hair was good for me, why wasn't it good for her? When she went grocery shopping, she put my taxi on the lower shelf of the basket trolley where I could watch humans go by. High-heeled shoes, cuffed and uncuffed pant legs, bare, hairy legs, silky smooth, nylon-wrapped legs, and spindly spandex-covered leggings all passed by, rushing to gather their food and hurry home. MM said she could be at home anywhere as long as I was around. She used my comfort as her timing aid. I heard her say to the check-out-clerk, "This is Kuan Yin, my shopper's helper. She keeps me from spending too much money. When her bladder gets full, we go home!"

Yes, she paid great attention to my bladder needs, stomach needs, and comfort needs. Indeed, she kept my "reading room" neat as a pin, fed and watered me at appropriate times, and brushed, hugged, and stroked me to my heart's content. I was fully aware, however, that in doing all this for me, she was fulfilling services she had given her children so many years ago. It became clear that, when she retired, she retreated to her home, which had become an empty refuge from her hurried, stressful world. I had come at the right time to help her transition from being a workaholic to becoming a contented writer and homemaker—all the while doing the tasks she knows so well how to do.

Besides enriching her soul, I came to fill the void she had lived in for nearly twenty years. I made her empty nest a quiet reserve instead of a lonely retreat. For years, she had left the house at sunup to drive across town for a demanding job. After a 12-hour day, she drove home again, often when the moon was up. There was no one applauding such diligence, and I showed her that projects and goals were empty without some form of appreciation. I taught her to live in the moment, to bask in the joy of the morning at the breakfast table on the balcony. We watched the birds flit from one branch to the other, and I sat on her lap as she sewed bright-colored beads on a purple lace bed jacket she planned to give to a friend. I gave her something on which to lavish her caring spirit.

In caring for me, she continued in a leadership role following her years in the school and community. In tending to my needs, she was fulfilling her role as nurturer as she had done with her own children—and the children of others—so many years ago. This time, I was giving back to her every moment of care that she gave me. Even in my physical need, I was, in fact, nurturing her.

Wardrobes for Saints, Goddesses, and Toxic Talismans

Historically, Maltese have been tolerant of exuberant companions who loved to dress their puppies in little outfits. As you may know, tolerance is one of our many virtues. I think when humans reach the "empty nest" stage, many bring an animal into their homes. Perhaps they fantasize about having a second chance to parent and, this time, doing it right. I suspect this dress-up ritual clearly indicates a human desire for real babies. Or maybe it is just a way to revert to one's own childhood.

"Let's play dolls!" Why else would grown-up people patiently brush hair, tie bows in our bangs, buy seasonal outfits, and shop for bonnets, sweaters, and boots? Why else do they coo and use baby language in sugary falsetto when they talk to us: "Do oo want to go potty?" "What a dood dirl!" "Koochie koochie koo," "Do oo want to go bye bye?"

Good Lord, we have enough trouble learning the basic vocabulary: *paper, toys, bed, dinner, bad,* and *good.* Actually, the latter two are simple. *Bad* is always coupled with an irate facial expression followed by a low, harsh tone of voice, and explicit body language like head waggling, finger pointing, and foot swinging. I take care to stay out of range when the foot starts to swing. Ask any dog. The term "bad dog" means withdrawal of affection, stomping of feet, yelling at the master's spouse, and vigorously indicating where the sports page is located.

On the other hand, "good dog" is said with spirited, high-keyed, rounded vocal tones and silken syllables as my Mistress clutches me to her bosom and coos and clucks over me like I had just made her day. When I get three "good dog" celebrations within a short period of time, MM calls all her friends to share the news as if they were dying to hear one more time how proud she is I came into her life. *Good* is definitely preferable to *Bad*. Yes, *Good* is definitely good.

It's so easy to digress when talking about humans; they are so interesting. Now where was I? Oh, yes, the wardrobe. I have told you about my Mistress driving to Julesburg to adopt me. I had no idea what a "to do" that event was. I hardly *knew* the woman before she had attached a cumbersome pink collar with rhinestones around my neck and dragged me out to the back yard for a photo session in the wind. How I hate the wind. My Mistress looked all misty-eyed as she posed with me for pictures that would rival those of the forthcoming grandchild. She held me every way except from my hind legs, just to capture my best side on film. I tolerated it until her friend presented her with a "baby shower gift." Oh, come on now, a baby shower for me?

My Mistress had made her friend wait for the entire one-hundred-and-fifty-mile trip before she finally opened this present. She loves suspense. "Good things are worth waiting for," she always says. She slowly unwrapped the package, making sure to fold the brilliant yellow paper carefully so she could reuse it on another present. Dr. Anderson agonized until MM finally opened the box. It revealed a shining red vinyl slicker, lined with matching plaid flannel. Dr. Anderson had made the outfit with her own hands.

Immediately MM fastened me into this restrictive garb and took more photos as if I were modeling for some nautical dog magazine. "Look, I'm going to sea!" I barked. Braving the prairie winds and unable to move while locked into the slicker, I fell over. My Mistress said it was like watching the old "Laugh In" television program with Artie Johnson falling off the park bench in slow motion. It was a humiliating experience. And she still took more photographs. "This one's for your baby book," she cooed.

That was my first experience with real clothing. I have since received a hand-me-down from Cecelia: a sky blue dress with matching bonnet trimmed with white eyelet. The dress had a pink monogram "Angel," another moniker I assume I was expected to grow into. (Actually, have you ever known someone named Angel who looked or acted like one?)

Cecelia's Mistress sometimes calls her Angel, but often she calls her CC, which is short for Cecelia Clarice. Can you imagine? My Mistress laughingly calls her *Saint* Cecelia. She probably thinks Cecelia is a saint because she is housebroken. Actually, Cecelia *is* an *avatar*—a goddess or special being reincarnated.

She is also some kind of fashion plate when it comes to canine apparel. I have heard endless telephone conversations about the Colorado Rockies outfit, but what really amazes me is CC's witches' costume. I saw her poised with pointed hat, shawl, and broom in paw!

She wore it for a photograph to be sent as a Halloween greeting card to the owner of the kennel from which we came. Indeed, I saw a whole closet full of clothes when I went to visit Dr. Anderson and Cecelia.

Once, at PetsMart, my Mistress was moved to buy me a bomber jacket. That's right! A brown, vinyl jacket with a fleece collar and cuffs. It felt much like the little red slicker, the gift Dr. Anderson gave me when I was just a wee thing. However, having gained a pound, I could now handle the stiff vinyl, and the fleece kept me cozy even if the wind blew. I never fell over in the wind again, for the belt kept the jacket neatly in place and I firmly stood my ground. Cecelia admired the jacket but felt her own *couturier* outfits were far superior to those garments bought off the rack.

Cecelia is a people name. Many dogs have people names. Bassets and hounds are often called such names as Dudley, Clarence, and George. I personally know a Bichon who answers to Boozer. He teaches his master, a Texas oilman, to slow down. In the wee hours, the man strokes Boozer, and they have a great talk. Boozer would like his master not to drink so much, and actually, when he is brushing Boozer, it's really hard to reach for another beer. And in the brushing session, he has no "deals" to make, no contracts to sign, and no one to impress.

People personify their animal companions with names like those when they need a buddy or a pal who puts no social obligation on them. I think they use people names because, when humans look into the animal's eyes, they see a reflection of their own soul. Dogs, and other animals, communicate directly from the soul. They must first get the attention of their humans, however, to see their eyes and to make the soul connection.

The Wind and the Rain

*"Look, I'm going to sea!" I barked. Braving the prairie winds
and unable to move while locked in my slicker, I fell over.*

That connection is crucial. Maybe you have never traveled in the wild before, but if you have, did an expert ever tell you not to make eye contact with the wild animals? They instruct you to look at something else, back away until you are out of sight, and move v-e-r-y slowly. That is because if a lion or bear or rhinoceros meets your eyes, he fixates on his dinner—you. Unlike a dog, which will go without dinner just to be by your side, wild beasts are unable to think about anything except immediate self-gratification. My Mistress says some people are just like that. Sometimes people take care of their own needs before they think of the needs of their animal companions. If people had any concern for soul, they would recognize it in these companions and make *their* needs top priority!

Speaking of priorities, dressing an animal may be fun for the human but not so much fun for the companion animal. Some like it, others don't. For example, you wouldn't get away with dressing up wild "dogs" like a dingo or a hyena. Only domesticated dogs have the patience to endure human attire. They have been around humans—as companions, as working and hunting comrades, and as household protectors—since the dawn of time.

In the vegetable world, on the other hand, that is a different matter. CC and I have heard tales that humans are especially silly about dressing little objects—roots of plants and dolls. CC found it interesting that, in primitive times, people actually dressed the human-shaped mandragora root in wisps of cloth. The mandragora appears to have arms and legs, a body and a head. Folklore says that the root agonizes when it is pulled out of the ground. Its scream drives people mad or puts them to death. For that reason, medieval people used a starving dog to pull the root out of the ground. They tied the dog to the hefty root and left food where the dog had to strain at the rope to reach it.

I told CC, "People dressed the deadly root to personalize it and give it a specific personality, usually of an enemy."

CC answered, "Just like that old root, I take on the personality of the costume I wear too."

I asked her how she felt when she was in witches' garb.

"I feel powerful," she said. "I feel like flying over to see you in your condominium. I think witches must have had fun!"

What a show dog! I told CC, "I think *those* witches were little old ladies who lived deep in the forest."

"What's a forest?" CC asked. "Do we have one near our penthouse?"

"These witches," I replied patiently returning to the subject, "dressed in tall black hats and black dresses like your Halloween garb. They had knowledge of healing and killing herbs found growing in nooks and crannies everywhere. They paid attention to the changing seasons, the cause of disease, and the effect of herbal mixtures that nobody else noticed."

"My Mistress notices everything," said CC, chasing through the rooms. "Do you think she's a witch?"

Ignoring her joke, I said, "Witches wrapped roots in a fashion similar to the patron's enemy, gave each root an appropriate name, and chanted incantations over it. Eventually, the patron's enemy, under the spell, would fall ill of a mysterious ailment and die."

"Oh," said CC, stopping her morning exercise rounds for a lap of water, "Dr. A. has a doll collection." She lapped up more water and said thoughtfully, "I am teaching her that dolls do not have a beating heart, understanding eyes, and a searching soul. I want her to treat every person the way she treats me, not the way she treats her dolls."

"Forgive me," she sighed, "dolls are just empty-headed playthings, but companion animals are *avatars*, gifts sent from Heaven."

"Hmm," I said, trying to stay on the subject, "I think *early chemists, fearfully labeled witches,* had a cottage industry, which made them lots of money from people who wanted to do evil things to their enemies or competitors. Evil intentions are expensive." CC allowed that Dr. Anderson had no such side income.

"Nevertheless," I told her, "most humans basically have good intentions, and I am growing used to the good intentions of mine, whom I adore—MM."

Travel is Travail

Travel is adventurous, exciting—and very tiring. Sometimes my Mistress disturbs my play by saying something like, "Are you ready to go bye bye?" Well, of course, I'm ready to go bye bye. Who wouldn't want to go to the park to play? Who wouldn't like to get out of the condo for a leisurely stroll in the greenbelt? Some creatures are literal shut-ins. The essence of their lives is limited. To get MM to take me out, I prance my puppy paws to the bone for hours chasing my pink rubber porcupine and pouncing on my squeaky hamburger, my gummy bone, and my rawhide.

Since I found this fuchsia treasure box filled with bouncing balls and other squeaky toys, I no longer have to stand on two hind legs at the door barrier gazing pathetically through the mesh. No longer must I just watch my Mistress read the Sunday paper before she bequeaths certain sections to the potty-liner stack. No longer do I have to dance from one side of the doorway to the other behind the "training gate," looking just like a miniature trained bear with pink bows in my topknot. I have diversion! I have entertainment!

Speaking of entertainment, I must say the dancing bear act certainly gives my Mistress a chuckle. Actually, that is another of my training strategies. In addition to that imploring look, the dancing bear routine often helps me get my way, for when I have danced enough, she rises from her studies and picks me up in her arms. I just stand on my hind legs and work my way around her chair or the bed, bobbing up and down to see over the cushions.

"You are so cute," she coos. She forgets she just yelled at me because I added a bark to my act. She pets me lovingly. She rubs my ears and my paws, my chin, and my tummy. When I stretch in appreciation, she massages my haunches, my back, and my shoulders with gentle vigor. With a little more practice, she will be a fine puppy masseuse. I will keep doing the dancing bear act to help her perfect her massage skill. MM is learning to relax. While massaging me, she thinks only of my comfort. I am teaching her that all creatures, animal companions, and people need time and attention. That is what she needs, too. By allowing her to focus on me, I focus on her. I am teaching her the qualities of unconditional love. She spends a great deal of time stroking me and I spend quality time soothing her. MM catches on fast. She knows that, when I dance like a tiny bear, I want attention.

She must have caught on to my "disruption of the reading" technique for, in a short while, this pink treasure chest appeared with new toys added to my collection. I think my Mistress would also buy lots of toys for her grandchildren if they would ever come to see her. She has drawers of crayons, colorful books, and puzzles I know are not intended for me. I just play with my tiny yellow rabbit she bought me at Easter instead of intruding into the belongings of others.

The Treasure Box

I prance my puppy paws to the bone for hours chasing my pink rubber porcupine and pouncing on my squeaky hamburger.

Just when I get used to amusing myself, she interrupts my play with an invitation to go out in the pet taxi. She is really into this potty training routine, so I oblige by filling up the sports page with appropriate social comment while she prepares the interior of the pet taxi to accommodate my amusement in transit. In goes the gummy bone. In goes the porcupine. With it goes the rawhide. "Hey," I bark, "you forgot my squeaky hamburger!"

Well, after elaborate preparations, she has filled the "diaper bag" with extra sports sections in case I need to step into the ladies' room to do some reading. She also includes extra food and water, my rhinestone leash, and some "cookies" I received for Christmas from Frannie, my cousin the miniature dachshund. No human baby has more emergency supplies than I.

Of course she includes the always-present camera. My Mistress must be practicing for a second career as a photojournalist, for we never go out without the camera. Traveling to the store means I snooze and wait patiently by her side as she shops for bread and milk and eggs. If she needs greater quantities of supplies, she leaves me home so she can carry everything up the three flights of stairs in one trip. She doesn't want me injured when she struggles up the stairs with an overload.

When I first arrived at her home, she was not used to juggling groceries, dry cleaning, diaper bag, purse, camera, and pet taxi. So now, I just about have her conditioned to let me play in peace at home with my toys when she has many things to carry upstairs. I have been unsuccessful, so far, in training her to make several trips, so I have trained her to shop for massive supplies on her own. She simply refuses to make several trips from the car, across the broad lawn, to her third-floor condominium. She would rather struggle with one large load than carry many small ones easily. Can you imagine how precarious is the trip up three flights of stairs? Can you see the plastic bags from the cleaning flutter at the front of the caged front door of the taxi while the paper grocery bag crumples noisily in my ear? Can you just see the camera bag and the purse bumping against the plastic walls of the taxi, and my Mistress struggling to remove the junk mail from the mailbox in wind and snow? I tell you, sometimes she is very hard to train.

Through focused eye contact, I *have* had more success training MM to make my travel to Fort Collins, Vail, and Aspen more enjoyable. If eye contact is not enough, I stand patiently aside until she asks me what we have forgotten for the long trip. Of course we have to endure the usual thirty-minute preparation ritual, the newspaper, the diaper bag, and the toys in the taxi. But I have her trained to cushion the taxi with my woolen lap robe and dress me in my lavender turtleneck sweater I received for Christmas. I particularly like that sweater because it isn't too tight. Sometimes the Colorado mountains can be cold, so when she pops out of the car to refuel it or herself, I can snuggle down into the woolly blanket and meditate. By doing nothing, one does everything. I have steadily trained her to slow down her pace another fifteen seconds. I patiently wait for her to explain to me where she is going and when she will return—something she had not done during her fifteen years of single life.

Over the course of time, she is changing. Sometimes she even seems anxious to tell me what we are going to do and whom we are going to see. Well, she just needs more gentle training to settle down. I wonder how other people feel when she is traveling by herself hither and yon without leaving even a name, a telephone number, or an address to contact in case of an emergency. After so many years of single living, she has guided herself and relied upon herself alone. Maybe it would be a good idea to communicate her plans to a friend or a family member. I think she needs a human confidante.

She does tell *me,* however. Everything. I listen for miles and miles to her chatter about where she is going, when she will return, why she is making the trip, whom she will meet, what she will wear, what she will say when she meets her friends, and other endless tidbits of information.

Just as the Goddess Kuan Yin sat on her paradise island of P'u T'o Shan answering every prayer addressed to her, I sit patiently, chin on paws. When I focus on the Goddess Kuan Yin as the symbol of human compassion and peace, I turn my mind away from my gummy bone and listen carefully to everything my mistress has to say. If the ancient Goddess Kuan Yin could give her ear to the weeping of the world, I can surely spend a few hours listening intently to the hopes and dreams, the consternations and prayers, of one middle-aged independent woman. The "good teacher" is available to all, using all situations and not wasting a thing. That is called Embodying the Light.

Besides, it is good therapy for MM. She is learning that if she does not trust people, she makes them untrustworthy. I perceive she feels safe with my comforting, compassion, and peacefulness. When we are alone, I send her messages through my thoughts and my very presence. I see she is shifting more toward trust and she is able to talk more freely than before. Focused listening brings greater awareness. We all learn from deeply listening to the wind, to the sounds of bees and crickets, to the silence of the forest, to the crashing of the waves on the rocks. We must become silent, slow our hearts, clear our minds of the mundane static surrounding us, and listen to the sounds of the universe.

That is how Goddess Kuan Yin listens. I just fix my round, black eyes intently on her face and move my head from side to side to let her know Kuan Yin empathizes with her. Like all good pupils, MM lives in a constant state of gratitude to her teacher. She cares very much about my messages and listens intently. Traveling with her is work, but enduring the preparations, hearing the constant monologue, and listening to the familial secrets is worth the effort to one who is born to be both comforter and confidante.

Please, Don't Even Mention It

The daily grooming, the play with the inflowing stream of tiny toys, the frequent games of hide-and-seek, and the short journeys to the supermarket, beauty salon, library, and bookstores grew even more pleasurable in the next couple of years. Our games gave MM more physical activity than she had before enjoyed. Picking up my papers in the "reading room" also allowed her to bend and stretch so, as she abhorred taking time to go to the gymnasium, I provided her with a moderate workout.

Once I recuperated from the first operation, I reached the stage of more adult pursuits. I was tired of sleeping on the cushion in the hallway since I was no longer a pup. Fully used to seeking out the papers in the "reading room," I deserved to be closer to MM.

One morning, I ventured to the foot of her huge bed and tried to get a look at her sleeping "way up there." She dropped a sleepy hand over the side of the bed and petted my head lovingly. That was nice. I began to play "dancing bear" bobbing up and down around the edge of the bed—just as I had done at the training gate, which had separated my long, empty hall from the rooms of the great Oriental carpets. Standing on my hind legs, I encircled the great brass bed and, as she saw my eager face bob into sight around the bed, I barked and she laughed.

"Oh, all right," she smiled, "just this once." As she scooped me up close to her, I realized how regal it felt to be up so high. There, I could look out of the window at the squirrels chasing each other on a branch. I could see the birds building their nests in the arms of the big pine tree. Out of that third-floor window, I could watch the rays of the sun play on the walls of the bedroom, casting beautiful shadows and intricate patterns as sunlight filtered through the treetops onto the lace curtains.

I watched the seasons change from this royal sleeping loft. Once I could see the heavens from atop the bed, I could take greater charge of watching over MM. Often in the middle of the night, she would awaken to find me sitting sphinx-like and gazing out at the moon and the stars. It reminded her it was never her intention to "allow a *dog*" on her pure, white bed, but once there, I would always remain. Well, almost always.

I could see I had become more than a canine companion to MM. Everyone learned to make invitations for both of us. If an invitation did not include me, she made excuses to stay home, preferring my company to that of many people she knew. She postponed trips when she realized I might not be welcome in a motel, and she declined to plan vacations to places where I would likely have to undergo quarantine. She actually hated to leave home . . . because *I* was there.

Instead, she was content to write in her studio as I sat patiently by. I had thoroughly trained her to take a break from the writing. When I began to see her shoulders sag or her

The Sentinel

Often in the middle of the night, she would awaken to find me sitting sphinx-like and gazing out at the moon and the stars.

posture slump from computer fatigue, I stepped out of my taxi and, sequentially stretching all my limbs, walked over to her chair. I steadily gazed at her until, finally aware of my presence, she would chuckle and lift me to her lap. I stared searchingly into her eyes to convey it was time to go down the spiral staircase to the rooms below. "Just a few more lines," she would say, then she hurriedly finished her thoughts. I would not, however, take my eyes from her face until she complied. She was becoming very compliant.

After my quick "read" of the sports page, we might sit quietly on the living room lounge listening to Baroque music while she groomed my fur. Comb and brush in hand, she would soothe me with pats and pets before she began to stroke my fur with the fine wire brush. Sometimes she would play "Roll Over" just so she could brush my soft underpinnings. Not overwhelmingly fond of that submissive posture and lying supine in her lap, I would not allow the brushing to begin until she had applied a reassuring massage. "Cleanliness is next to godliness," she would whisper. I, on the other hand, felt my *goddessness* came first.

In one of those grooming sessions, MM noticed how tender my hindquarters had become. She puzzled over my occasional flinch when she combed my left hind leg. She wondered why I pulled away from her when she tried to fluff my little tail. An animal's tail, you must know, acts like the flag on a ship. It sends a message to those who would know about the weather, the emotions, and the state of wellness. When I hold my little flag high, its silken strands streaming over my back, it is a fair day and I feel fine!

One day, though, she saw me protecting a bruise on that tender quarter as I lay curled up on the cushion. Her quick examination led us to take off and see the veterinarian immediately. He explained that the faces of many dogs are tear-stained because the little ducts are so tiny, they cannot drain the tears down inside the nose. That was true of my own eyes—*ahem—and* my anal gland.

Downsizing and in-breeding caused my kneecaps to be too small, too. "She has luxating patellas," he declared. That means when the parts of the knees don't fit, when the sockets of the leg don't support the kneecap, the patellas move about. Then the legs wobble and get weak. One day, he said, I might need to have surgery to keep from having a crippled gait—but not yet.

The doctor looked at my Mistress' anxious expression and said definitively, "Kuan Yin appears to have a ruptured anal gland." Well, not only was that painful for me to bear, but it was painfully embarrassing, too. MM again handed over my taxi to the veterinarian, and, trembling, made the arrangements for my surgery. After surgery, I was again relegated to the big cushion on the floor near MM's bed. But when the wound healed and the groomer worked her special magic on my blood-matted fur, I returned to the heights of the big bed and the comfort of MM's reassuring touch. Finally, as I quickly healed, I returned to my position of authority. Assuming my posture of inner vision during the night watch, I stayed stationed at my command post. From there, I could bound down the bed steps to attend to the door bell, the dryer buzzer, or the alarm clock. On my return, I would take a drink of water, nibble a little breakfast from my crystal dish in the dining room, or play with my toys. I was—once again—home.

People and Parties: Silver Slippers and Combat Boots

My Mistress is a gregarious sort who likes to invite family and friends to her home. It doesn't matter what the occasion, any excuse will do. Whether it's for breakfast, brunch, lunch, dinner, or supper, she likes to invite people over to eat. "A meal," she has said, "is a social event." To her, nibbling from the feedbag like racehorses do or grazing on grass like cattle and reindeer do or grabbing a kibble on the run as Maltese and other small canines do does not constitute a real meal. Unlike many modern people, MM thinks people should sit down at a well-set table, converse pleasantly, and enjoy every bite of a thoughtfully prepared meal.

When she's preparing the meal, she bounds around the house like an energetic Amazon, cleaning the china and the crystal, mourning over the stems unfit to put on the table. She says when people help her with the table clearing and "the washing up," as the British say, they are not careful. Once, some dear friends put her crystal goblets in the dishwasher. The new crystal was not tempered, so when she unloaded the dishwasher, she discovered that her whole new set of goblets was chipped. Of course, she said nothing to the guests, but *I* get to hear *all* about it each time she prepares to lay out a feast. She tells me everything, and I can assure you she would rather commit *hara-kiri* than allow others to help clear the table. Like Wonder Woman, she insists on doing it all herself.

She sets the table days in advance, covers it with a sheet to keep the dust off, and attacks the many labors-of-love by preparing long lists of menus, ingredient needs, and tasks to be done before the great event. That's when her beloved sons, her perfect grandchildren, or her intimate friends will each cheerfully poise two shoes underneath the table, awaiting the culinary surprises sure to delight. I, for one, am careful to avoid those dangerous, unpredictable shoes. Despite my desperate hunt for disregarded food flakes that inevitably find their way to the carpet, I wait until the guests are gone before I set out on my supper safari.

Weeks ahead of the dinner event, my Mistress gathers her cookbooks around her on the floor and thumbs through dozens of recipes that have taunted her taste buds and tormented her memory. When she has exhausted the cookbooks, she digs out several cooking magazines to which she subscribes. Oh, it makes my mouth water to see brisket of beef, steak tartar, and a gleaming pork roast in living color on the covers of these beautifully illustrated gourmet periodicals stacked in proud pillars around the kitchen. I am, however, not allowed to "read" the cookbooks as I "read" the sports pages located now in the laundry room. My social comment must be restricted to longing looks, respectful gasps, and tiny secret licks to the pictorial roast beef. I try to look disapprovingly at exotic ingredients such as "cellophane" noodles, jalapeños, and artichokes, but my efforts are lost when she gets focused elsewhere.

"Hmmm," she says, "this dish does look intriguing." She keeps thumbing through the pages engrossed, much like reading something I consider far more enlightening such as *my* magazine, *Dog Fancy*™, from PetsMart™.

The secret to her successful parties fascinates me. She formulates a menu of exotic dishes and then asks, "I wonder who would eat this spicy dish or that exotic fruit." I tell you, if only she would stick with meats and gravies, all *my* friends in town would turn out in hoards. Her friends probably would, too. But she says some of her friends are allergic to all kinds of foods, so choosing the menu first pleases *her* palate and serves as a guideline for the invitations. I guess if one were going to spend hours and a small fortune planning and preparing a meal, one should please one's self. I notice that her friends who applaud her Oriental cuisine get invited more often than her meat-medium-rare friends. I throw my vote in with the latter. I do not think goddesses *ever* eat food laced with soy, fish, oyster, or sesame, such as *lee kum kee*, *hoisin*, or other exotic sauces.

To tell the truth, the planning time is the most enjoyable for me, for I can curl up next to her on the lounge while she peruses the magazine pages and I can dream of roast duck, poached salmon, and grilled pork chops to my heart's content. But when the planning period is over, I really have to watch my step.

"Step" is the magic word. That's right. Could you imagine me flatter than a house-brand hamburger patty? I would be waffle-printed by her "birkies," Birkenstock™ shoes. I do like to stay near the kitchen counter, of course, to wait in anticipation of a chance morsel that occasionally sails across the counter as she wields her kitchen tools. Once, oh heart's delight, I witnessed a crumb of cheese drop toward the floor amidst a flurry of activity "way up there" on the counter. To my utter disappointment, she caught the creamy crumb in mid-flight before I had a chance to even salivate properly. If she wonders what doggie dreams I harbor, it is that one day I will catch a tad of turkey, a bit of bread, or a stir-fried tissue-paper-thin slice of steak before her eagle eye and agile hand can intervene. "Oo," she coos, "that's not *good* for doggies. We don't want you to *get sick*, Sweetie."

You know, if it is so bad for dogs, I wonder why she hasn't figured out it is probably not good for humans, either. I wonder why she doesn't quit this whirling dervish activity of meal preparation and just invite the gang over to share some of my crunchy Eukanuba™. There's plenty in my bowl to share. She says, "That's good for you!" Well, if it's good for *me,* why isn't it good for *her* too? Now, don't tell me that humans are carnivores and need their protein. All of my Mistress' vegetarian cookbooks stress how good grains and stuff that just *tastes* like meat is for humans. Now, *I* believe that humans are omnivores (Have-Teeth-Will-Eat-Anything). It seems more likely *they* would enjoy eating grain-and-sauce-food-in-a-bag, and we dogs, who *are* carnivores, would profit from eating *real meat*. If she likes to cook so much, she could whip up a leg of lamb for me any time.

Digestion and heart attacks notwithstanding, death could come just as easily from a careless sandal planted squarely on one's back as from a loving lick of an empty tuna can.

Um, succulent lamb, defatted, rolled, filled with garlic buds, and tied into a tidy roast. Beautiful, bountiful lamb, served with just a bit of rosemary and a little mint jelly, is pure epicurean joy. The smells wafting through the house make me dream of days of old when the lamb was sacrificed to the gods. The gods knew what was good. Added to that, MM loves to snip herbs from her wee herbal garden growing in huge pots that grace the railing of her balcony. Oregano, sage, chives, rosemary, chervil, and a variety of mint thrive in bountiful clusters just waiting for a roast, salad, or dessert to adorn.

When my Mistress is cooking, I have learned to move like a hummingbird, watching Her Worship's path while keeping a keen eye out for a floating Doritos™ chip. Her path, however, is more like a rocking motion of the quickstep. That is, just when I think she's going forward, she remembers one more thing she needs from the refrigerator. Then, rocking backward, she narrowly misses stepping on my pretty little tail. She does a lot of this kind of dance in what she calls a "boxcar kitchen" in the world's smallest condominium. I tell you, it's hard to figure her out.

She does warn me sometimes, however. When she's going to pull out a bottom drawer or sees she is getting in my way, she singsongs "toot-toot" so I am aware we are frantically crossing paths. Courteous guests who plod around our house could surely use her considerate, cheery little singsong. I can never tell what *they* are doing. For all I know, they are stalking me, waiting to whisk me up in their arms and smother me with kisses.

Sometimes an eleven-year-old girl, MM's beautiful granddaughter, lies in wait around the corner, ready to *pounce* on me at the first opportunity so she can brush my hair, wash my face, or clamp different kinds of miserable plastic bows in my topknot. If only *she* would chortle "toot-toot," I would head for my pet taxi posthaste. I know my job is to amuse grandchildren like her. Thank goodness MM's other grandchild is still in swaddling clothes.

Actually, age has little to do with the stalking admirer. My Mistress once invited two ladies, a generation apart, to come to brunch and enjoy my healing presence. The one who is nearer to eighty than she would like to admit competed with the lady who is closer to ninety-three than *she* will acknowledge. MM told me they both wanted to play Empress and hold me in their laps, stroking my silken hair to lower their blood pressure. To be sure, I gladly complied. I gave them my "adorable look" and captured their hearts. They sat still, handled me very gently, and never once pulled my hair. Actually, others are often gentle with me, too.

A soft-spoken southern lady named Mrs. Le Blanc likes to dress me up in Cecelia's old "Angel" dress with the matching bonnet. She is kind and gentle; I tolerate *her* grooming well, for I can tell she comes from a long line of dog lovers and doll dressers. People from the Old South talk kindly, slowly, and melodiously. She doesn't say "toot-toot," but she does drawl, "Look out now, little 'un, I'm a-goin' over yonder. Be careful, y' hear?"

Once the guests leave, I am exhausted. For weeks, I have dodged my Mistress' "birkies" during the preparation period and her high heels during the party. I have dodged her friends' sandals, wedgies, and espadrilles. I have avoided Rockports™ and Adidas™, and I have quickly hidden from construction boots and wingtips, alike.

The most fearsome of all are wingtips. "Oo, ow." It hurts just to think of the consequences if I take life too easy sitting near people's feet at parties. Whether their shoes are silver slippers or patent pumps, saddle shoes or spiked heels, all are stuff of terrible calamity. I wonder that, in their haste, humans don't trample their children! Frankly, I like

Dinner Party Dangers

I have learned from keen observation about human unawareness.
I advise humans to pay attention to where they put their spiked heels.

the Japanese custom of removing the shoes as one enters the house. It certainly keeps our Oriental carpets cleaner, but mostly, it removes the fear of impalement from my tiny heart.

My worst dream is that one day I am trapped in the middle of a ballroom on which gowned women and tuxedoed men glide across a polished floor. In slow motion, each tramples my fragile struggling little carcass as I try to activate paws that will not move. I imagine you have seen other dogs lying in front of the fire, sleeping soundly. In the midst of calm and repose, they suddenly jerk their feet, twitch, and whimper. They are experiencing my dream! To valiantly move paws but not be able to escape harm is everybody's nightmare. I have heard that humans have such dreams. MM has told me that sometimes people dream they are being chased by a beast that gains distance on them because they cannot move their feet fast enough. I think the pressures of unnecessary activity, unrealistic time schedules and deadlines, and unfounded anxiety cause such dreams. As busy as she is, MM would protect me, I know. After dessert when people linger over coffee or after dinner drinks, she puts me in her lap and strokes me rather than allow me to become entangled in crossed ankles and shuffling soles. She makes sure no one in MM's household would ever step on her darling.

I have learned from keen observation about human unawareness. I advise humans to pay attention to where they put their spiked heels and steeled toes. I warn them to give their animal companion a wide enough berth to escape disaster. And if dogs and cats could read, I would create a sign to say, "Stay clear of human feet!" As one works the crowd, it is better to warm laps than sniff the dainty powdered and enameled toes of lovely ladies.

Nothing Seems to Fit

Sleeping on MM's big bed was a responsibility as well as a treat but it was not meant to last. In January, my kneecaps indeed proved to be a worry. I slipped down the comforter of the great bed when I missed the landing of the bed steps. I had difficulty walking unassisted down the long tile hallway between the bedroom and the kitchen. I used the wall to lean on. Unless I had a burst of adrenaline inspired by the sound of MM coming up the stairs, I spent my time on the big cushions. MM had placed dozens of them throughout the house.

I seldom felt like running after my ball and I rarely played "the dancing bear." Amazingly, I no longer enjoyed standing on hind legs and peering out the glass at the sassy brown squirrel that had learned to taunt me. Next I knew, MM took me back to the veterinarian. "We have been afraid this would happen," he said. "It certainly is a case for the specialist."

An orthopedic surgeon was immediately assigned to get my legs back in working order. First, he would have to make the knee sockets larger to allow the kneecaps to rock properly. He would move muscles around the new position and tendons, too. He would pin the tendons in place to support the new configuration. Bones, muscles, fascia, and tendons were all involved. For the specialist, this was just a routine operation. "She is such a young dog," he said, "and healthy. She'll go through this just fine. These little fellows bounce right back. It's much harder on the bigger dogs."

My Mistress hesitated to let me go. She had only planned on my regular teeth cleaning; needing knee surgery, although expected *someday*, came as a surprise. She carefully inquired about the procedure, the care, the period of recuperation, and my general condition. The doctor and the specialist reassured us I would be back to normal within a few weeks.

When my Mistress picked me up from the hospital, she worried about how I would get to my food and water. She worried, too, about how I could manage "the paper in the reading room" without the use of my hind legs. Surprisingly, the doctors had decided to repair *both* legs instead of correcting just one and cleaning my teeth. In addition, they wanted to get both knees in working order at one time, for anesthesia is always an ordeal. They also believed the teeth-cleaning procedure would be too hard on my system. The teeth could wait.

MM watched as I dragged myself from the cushion to the paper in the next room. She followed me to assist in whatever way she could. When she saw me trying to urinate by standing on my front paws, she cradled my body with her hands. Of course, that didn't work with me. Not only could I *not* get the right muscles to work, but also I had to have the privacy of my endeavors. For a few days, MM had to allow me to manage in my own way and follow up with a warm rinse in the sink. Slowly, I was able to manage the proper stance and support my weight with all my legs. Many times I have wondered how humans get along with only two!

Recuperation was a struggle. MM had taken a few days off work and kept me close to her. With incisions on both kneecaps, they were readily accessible to my curiosity. My Mistress watched carefully to be sure I would let the knees heal without scratching them. Instead of tying on the big white sock, which would hobble my legs, MM dressed me in Cecelia's Angel gown to cover the stitches. It reminded me of when she drove to Nebraska to get me and we struggled in the wind to take a photograph in the red slicker. When CC gave me the little blue dress with "Angel" embroidered on it, I thought it was intrusive. It hung down over my knees and inhibited my running. But during my recovery, I found the soft fabric that covered my incisions very comforting.

MM cared for me like a baby. She held me in her lap and rocked me to sleep. She is a tender soul. I realized more and more how acutely she had suffered behind the Wonder Woman façade. She flew with the heart of an eagle but had the soul of a turtledove. She never allowed her feelings to roam freely. She held them in and they became secondary to her career. She always strived to be productive, efficient, and organized when she should have been focusing on her tattered soul. From the Tao, we learn that the master, or mistress, sees things as they are, without trying to control them. They let them go their own way and reside at the center of the circle. MM had not ridden in the center of the circle.

Her constant *doing* got in the way of her *being*. I have been teaching her to do her work, and then step back. That step is the only Path to Serenity.

My maladies in an earthly guise as a beautiful canine have brought out the tenderness in her. At night when I could no longer keep my eyes open, she gently massaged my knees and worked the joints to rehabilitate the muscles. She kept me under close scrutiny and took me to the doctor for checkups to be sure I was healing properly.

The first visit was to remove the exterior stitches I had been unable to loosen and to check the cyst that had formed around an internal stitch. The second visit was a checkup after the first month. The stitches had healed completely, but I still had not returned to my former energy and enthusiasm. Later, I also visited the specialist who took X-rays and pronounced a complete healing from the surgery. In spite of the doctors' optimism, I was not well. MM began to worry deeply when, after two months, she again saw me leaning against the wall to walk. I realized that the earthly body I had selected in this incarnation was frail and fragile. I won't be making that mistake again.

MM took me to the veterinarian again. He tested the reflexes in my legs. They did not respond properly. She was beside herself when I showed a greater need to sleep during the day. I also failed to show interest in the bells and buzzers, and could not walk without help from the wall. When she saw that incontinence was increasing, she called the doctor. He was attending a seminar, they said. He would return in a week and a half. An aide had said that the incontinence probably happened because I had forgotten my training in the long convalescent period. Some expert!

MM had seen me struggle and fail to adjust my weight and rearrange my body on the big cushion so my head did not hang over it on the floor. Her total frustration manifested into despair as she saw my health was steadily getting worse. In fact, I was unable to do much more than eat and sleep. I welcomed her cradling me in her arms like a tiny baby. While I would never have allowed myself to be held with my spine in her arms when I was just a puppy, I now sank deeply into her cradling lap. I allowed her to rock me and comfort me with her soft, calm voice. I cherished her warmth, and she mine. Her nourishing without possessing, her selfless behavior without expectations, brought her closer and closer to virtue.

Kuan Yin's Commandments to New Mistresses

After three years of communicating, both through experience and thought, my Mistress and I have compared and contrasted the upbringing of children and pets. Just as some people enjoy "selective hearing," my Mistress and I have developed a Selective List of Commandments for rearing small creatures. We say *rearing* because, if you recall from freshman English, one raises cabbages and Hell, but one rears children. My Mistress says rearing is like a warm and cuddly hen settling her heft upon a nest to incubate, protect, and communicate with her young. Heft, I assume, is her synonym for rear. That is not to say one rears her children by sitting on them.

Not to belabor the point, here are the Seven Commandments we created:

I

Feed the Bears Good Food

Bears need to be able to live in the wild. They need appropriate food. As a matter of fact, they may think of *people* as food. Bears and other wildlife thrive on natural foods like berries and fish, but when times get tough, they will come into human communities and resort to eating trash. Likewise, what puppies need to grow healthy and strong is Eukanuba™ or some other quality baby dog food. Feeding spaghetti leftovers and other scraps to your pets is a lazy way to nourish them. Last night's Thai noodle soup is today's garbage. If it is not good enough for your table, it certainly is not good enough for the dog dish. Treat your animal companions right! Their health and well being depend on you.

II
Exotic Food is For the Birds

Trying out new recipes on the dog the day before your company arrives is the wrong approach. Wait. If the company doesn't convulse with stomach pains—or die—the new dish might be safe for the dog. Still, people food is better for people. Animals need a diet that will keep them fit to run and play, to work and protect. *Tabouli* and *cous cous* probably will not get them through the day.

Animal companions cannot brush their teeth every day. You may have to do that for them. Crunchy food, designed to keep the teeth and gums healthy, should be the staple in a dog's diet. Mushy foods like crab soufflé speed decay. To clean an animal's teeth, the veterinarian needs to anesthetize it. Anesthesia cannot be good for tiny creatures. Providing good nutrition for you and for your animal companion is up to you; both need to crunch a bunch to stay healthy.

III
Teach Animal Companions to be Well Behaved

Unless they are entertainers, dogs do not need to overextend their haunches just to provide your friends with a laugh. Instead of teaching them useless tricks to impress your friends, teach dogs good manners that will keep them safe and acceptable to all others in the animal kingdom. My Mistress has said "Good manners are treasures to the young." I say they are a comfort to the old. Appropriate behavior will make both dogs and children welcome visitors even in the palaces of queens and kings. For example, parakeets, Rottweilers, and children should not be allowed to carry food onto the Oriental carpet, nor should they be allowed to squawk, growl, or bellow at visitors. More importantly, as an owner or a parent, *you* have the responsibility to train them to identify and use their private *toilet*. Train them never, never to void or evacuate on a neighbor's shoulder, shoe, or lap. That makes for rude stains and lasting enemies! They must become educated enough to know the difference between sports pages and shoulder pads. The master or mistress is a trusted teacher, the lead dog in the canine world.

IV
Food and Love Build Strong Bones

Food, affection, and purpose are as important to lap dogs as they are to children. They require hugs every day—part of the nutritional needs of all domesticated beings including wives and husbands. Dogs, like people, thrive on the praise of a job well done.

They enjoy the value you place on your positive, appropriate expectation of excellence. Too many animal companions and children grow up learning mediocre standards, insufficient values, and rude manners. As a result, low self-esteem becomes an issue. Children and dogs must have parameters.

Establishing boundaries is a part of being a parent or a pet owner. When children and pets accomplish expectations and respect boundaries, they understand their appropriate roles. Esteem follows; it comes from pride in performance. My Mistress and I believe poor training brings disgrace to the mistress and the parent. To be honest, a lack of good manners is a crucial, cultural crisis.

If you are unwilling to invest the time, patience, commitment, and *personal* involvement required to train a creature—whether dog, iguana, or child—do not have one! Don't rely on hiring an obedience trainer to have an obedient dog; your companion animal will always think of the trainer as mistress or master and may not obey *your* commands. Conversely, don't rely on the values, mores, standards, or expectations of a nanny or child care attendant to teach those virtues to your child. The child may behave like a sophisticated lap dog at the baby-sitter's house and like a savage beast in your company.

V

Reward Small Achievements with Small Treats

Administer the gift of a kibble for kibble-sized performances and give large bones for real heroics. Receiving huge gifts for low performance overwhelms puppies and children.

This indicates mistress/parent frustration at their own inadequacy to train them properly. My Mistress calls this over-generous behavior the syndrome of the "Disneyland Daddy" or the "Malibu Mamma." When fledglings are given too large a treat, they undervalue truly excellent behavior and expect more and more for less and less.

For instance, my Mistress has said that paying children to go to school is a good example of this devaluation of effort. It is a politician's desperate ploy to reduce the dropout rate! One must be mature to be a good mistress, a good teacher, or a good parent. It is best to understand that the expectation of standards, adequate praise, self-respect—plus the rewards of a good education—are, in and of themselves, of greater value than money. What the world needs is better parenting, better parenting, and better parenting.

VI
Miracles, Too Great an Expectation

Each breed has unique characteristics. Lap dogs, although they have great hearts, cannot retrieve ducks from the pond nor guard a junkyard with intimidation and credibility. Conversely, Saint Bernards, kind and gentle as they may be, cannot sit for hours in your lap. Nor can Pit Bulls comfort you in silence with soft, adoring eyes from the end of the satin comforter.

Dogs and children were bred and born with special assets. Each has outstanding abilities. Mistresses and masters, like good parents, must discover and develop those inborn traits, value their worth, and celebrate their achievement. They must never punish an animal or a child for what she or he cannot be.

For example, gardeners cannot expect Spaniels—born to dig—to honor the purple climatas and the dazzling daffodil. Potters and ceramists cannot discipline a large dog for wagging a long, brushy tail in their studio of fine, fragile porcelain, fresh from the kiln. Similarly, hunters cannot expect Yorkies and Shih Tzus to do water retrieval work for which even French poodles were bred. Understand and honor chromosomes; choose selectively the breed that will meet your needs—and whose needs you can meet—and then expect the best of what each can do.

VII

Model Behavior For Dogs and Children

Just as parents must model the good behavior they expect from their children, mistresses and masters must model, through leadership, the behavior they expect of their puppies. For example, one cannot expect calm and kindly reactions from a dog when the masters themselves race to the door grumbling and cursing at the ring of the doorbell. Dogs, like children, sense and imitate the nervous, irrational, and hyperkinetic reactions of their mistresses and parents, respectively—just as they mirror their demeanor when faced with crisis. Mistresses, masters, and parents have a responsibility to model *appropriate* behavior to fit the circumstance. Yet if one cannot direct and control oneself, how can one control a dog or a child?

Teach your dogs to bark at intruders and sit quietly for company. Teach them to be cautious of strangers, yet accepting of friends. A mistress must, in the mind of the dog, *be* the "Lead Dog." That is, to gain respect, you must take the lead—and not allow dogs and undisciplined youth to run your household. If such a creature is required, however, one can always buy a cat or suffer life with an immature tyrant.

Conversely, MM has said *parents* must model for the children, not the other way around. Since a full generation of parent-children has grown up in the "Me Generation," it has created children with no childhood and parents with no responsibilities! Training dogs or children is a labor of love, but, to quote Shakespeare, "'tis one." Both require hard work. Both are well worth the effort.

Conclusion

Well, there you have it. My Mistress and I have been together just three short years and, during that time, we have formulated these Seven Commandments. They are the keys to success. And if you want a good relationship, you must learn to relate. Indeed, if you want a wife, you must be willing to be a good husband. If you want children, you must be willing to sacrifice, model, and teach good values. And if you want a dog, you must not only tend, train, and love, but also lead. If you are not prepared to listen to the wisdom of the ages, make sacrifices, spend time, and give to others, then allow yourself time to grow up until you do understand.

All creatures—cats, dogs, ferrets, and other domesticated animals—need food, love, and reasonable expectations. They also need appropriate parameters. Children, too, need boundaries to help them understand what is expected of them. Good breeding and good training lead to full understanding and harmony.

I, Kuan Yin, have three basic things to teach: simplicity, patience, and compassion. That means keep the training simple, be patient and consistent, and by all means be compassionate. Your animal companions will tell you with their eyes how much they love to be with you, how much they trust you, and how much they are willing to sacrifice for your well-being. Remember that the *soft* overcomes the *hard*. Your loving training will pay off in eternal harmony.

The Final Analysis

No sooner had I completed writing my Commandments to people who want an animal companion than MM had to call the veterinarian again. Her manner was far from soft and calm. Because our doctor was out of town, MM needed to find someone else in the practice. An inexperienced colleague answered the telephone. My Mistress would not allow me to be examined and reexamined by the person who had thought all along my incontinence was a sign of disobedience. In quiet desperation, she called the Veterinary Teaching Hospital in Fort Collins and took the first appointment available the next Tuesday. The drive would be two hours long. She would arise at 4:30 a.m. as she had always done before I arrived in her life. She held me close and told me we would soon go bye-bye to get some help. We spent most of the night cuddling and rocking in the lounge. I slept a deep, quiet sleep. I deeply concentrated on my mission here on earth. I had chosen this woman whose spirit had been dying. Her solitude, her loneliness, and her diminished lack of purpose needed a boost to get her back on the path. She had at last found something to love—me—and she took charge of my care.

Monday was difficult for MM. She canceled all her appointments for Tuesday before she finished up her Monday meetings. It was unfortunate she had arrived home late, for I had called out to her during the day. Trapped in this frail Maltese body, I, the comforter, needed *her* comfort. When she came to the door, she inserted the key and, as was her habit, rang the door chimes. She came in quietly and called my name, expecting the usual reception of rowdy barking, joyful "little bear" jumping, and the usual "hurrah" of delighted greeting. This day, unable to pull myself together, I struggled to reach her. She called my name again. With a mighty burst of adrenaline, I raced down the hall toward her. I saw the look on her face as I lost control, fell on my side, and went into an episode of uncontrollable running actions with my immobile hind legs. The terrible dream of the shiny dance floor with ladies spiked heels and gentlemen's patent leather pumps returned for real.

"Oh, God! Oh, God, please no," she cried.

She knelt down and picked me up, called my name, and held me close. My body calmed; she stroked me gently. Soon I became uncomfortable and she set me on the carpet to let me recuperate. It was then she saw I had completely lost control, not only of my hind legs but also of my forepaws. She immediately put me in my taxi. It was cold and windy outside, but she wasted no time maneuvering her way through the rush-hour traffic to the emergency room of the veterinary hospital across town. Quietly driving through the wind and the rain, she kept up a constant *mantra* of supplication.

"Please, God, not now." She felt my spirit oozing away and she anticipated the unthinkable. She began to grieve at the very thought of my departure.

The Nightmare

The terrible dream of the shiny dance floor with ladies' spiked heels and gentlemen's patent leather pumps returned for real.

At that late hour, a doctor quickly took us to a quiet room and put me gently on a sheepskin mat to examine me. He remarked on the wonderful condition of my fur and my body as he stroked me reassuringly. My Mistress sighed in hopeless distress, then sobbed softly but uncontrollably. After a thorough examination, the doctor said he would keep me overnight for observation until a neurologist could examine me in the morning. Although I had no temperature, he could see I was very ill. He thought that in my distress during the afternoon, I had likely not taken in food and water, so he planned to administer fluids. He assured MM he would not allow me to suffer pain. He promised to call her periodically throughout the night and let her know of my progress. He was confident that I would feel better in the morning.

"We were sure the problem had been the kneecaps," he said. "Undoubtedly, the knees and other symptoms have masked the real problem. I suspect that to be neurological. We'll check with the specialist in the morning. Her reflexes should respond to this test." He demonstrated the test of rubbing my legs on the edge of the table.

"She should immediately withdraw the legs," he said. But I didn't.

For nearly a half an hour, my Mistress held me in her lap as the veterinarian busied himself with preparations for blood tests and a telephone call to the neurologist. My Mistress, who always rose to the challenge when courage was required, sat like a silent tower of strength as she rocked me, stroked me, and talked softly to me. She reluctantly let me go when Atom, the veterinarian's assistant with a cosmic name, come to take me to my room at the hospital. There, the veterinarian made a nest of sheepskin for me and administered fluids to my traumatized body. MM took care of the ubiquitous paperwork and went home to worry—and to mourn.

Atom laid me gently in an observation kennel and turned to tend to other animal companions who were recuperating from various maladies. Actually, I no longer needed his attention. My body was there, but slowly I began to prepare for a long journey to be assigned in the early morning hours. My spirit tried to call out to MM, but she could not hear. She was in the parking lot struggling through her tears to see the ignition switch on her car. In my thoughts, I tried to tell her I was being called to move forward to develop another soul. I tried to tell her that each separate being in the universe returns to the Common Source. The ancients knew that returning to the Source is serenity. My time with her had been rich with meaning and with love, and my Source was calling me to other tasks. MM would come to understand that as mistress, she must stay behind; that is why she will move ahead. She will learn to be detached from all things; that is why she will be one with them. She will learn to let go of herself and will soon be perfectly fulfilled.

Early in the morning, the very morning I was to have gone to the Veterinary Medicine doctors at Colorado State University, I left the soft white heap that once was my body.

I was galloping as fast as my paws would take me through the Great Halls and Steep Stairs toward the Golden White Light that called me gently but firmly. As my mind dashed through a series of rainbows, my beautiful corkscrew tail, fully unfurled, waved a fond farewell to MM who had by now received the final telephone call from the emergency room doctor. She had been a good mistress—had learned her lessons well. Her loving nature had fully re-emerged;

therefore my mission with her was finished. The hardest lesson of all would be the reality that one has but does not *possess* anything. Parents, spouses, children *all* eventually return to their Source. Nothing is forever. My body was leaving but my spirit would always remain.

I will return from time to time in her pleasant dreams. On a summer's night when the moon is full or at dawn on a clear, spring day when the squirrels peek cautiously into the bedroom window, my spirit will sit motionless on MM's bed. It will gaze approvingly at the peaceful smile on her lips as she recalls the picnics, the parties, and the many friends we two had shared. She'll be all right now that she has remembered how to love unconditionally. MM will make herself available to all people and will not reject anyone. She will soon be ready to use all situations for good and not waste any opportunity to teach and to serve. This is called Embodying the Light.

I had to move quickly, for I had work to do. Somewhere a soul was dying, and I was called to comfort and bring joy back into another person's life. The man had lost his wife, his business, and his brave heart. I knew what he needed was a loving Airedale to guide him through these terrible times. As an *avatar*, I knew I could assume whatever form I needed for the mission. Yes, an Airedale would do nicely. With him, we would enjoy runs in the park, fly-fishing trips on the Colorado River, and jogging along the highway as he trained for another marathon. Most certainly he would insist on the mandatory obedience school for such a frisky companion. But there would also be lounging on an Indian carpet in front of the fireplace in winter and daring fetes in the summer with this man who had become so success-driven that he had forgotten how to express his love.

The Transition

As my mind dashed through a series of rainbows, my beautiful corkscrew tail, fully unfurled, waved a fond farewell to MM . . .

As with MM, I would teach him that loving is more than mere words. With time to scratch my ears and the responsibility to groom my fuzzy Airedale fur, I would teach him to *show* love, not just *mouth* it. This time, though, I vowed to choose a form that had stronger knees and sturdier ductwork.

Wind, the Harbinger of Change and Growth

You are now hearing the voice of MM. Kuan Yin cannot complete this story. Her mission accomplished, she was called to move on to comfort other human charges. Who knows in what form she will return? Yet, in the three and a half years I was privileged to welcome her into my life, I experienced greater joy than I had ever known as a single adult. It is strange to say why an animal fills a gap other humans can never hope to fill. Some people have never experienced intense love from others. In their minds, no one—not children, spouse, nor friends—have given or could give them unconditional love. "Concerning love," Kuan Yin has said, "One must give and one must receive." To be able to receive is to honor the giver.

Perhaps some people have not felt loved because they thought they were unworthy of it. In human relations, competition, and conflict, misunderstanding and hurt feelings exist. Struggling with *ego*, humans remain concerned with fulfilling their own needs. They do not compete with one's dog or cat; they only learn from their animal companions if they allow the lessons.

While some humans are oblivious to the subtle changes in others, they notice every movement made by loving pets. Kuan Yin gave me her full attention. She looked into my eyes when I talked to her. Her focus made me feel that she was listening intently to every word I said. I felt that she absorbed my feelings and transmitted her thoughts to mine through her eyes. They never left mine. I never felt alone when she was with me. Although she never voiced a word, I felt her telling me that *ordinary* people reject solitude. I had long known the difference between loneliness and solitude. When people feel lonely, they crave connection with others. They feel uncomfortable in their own company. On the other hand, solitude brings an opportunity to enjoy quiet moments of reading, long hours of writing, a weekend of gardening, time to think and reflect, and, Kuan Yin added, "time to connect with the Oneness of the universe."

My puppy (for I have always considered Kuan Yin a baby) gave unconditional love. She was another set of eyes and another beating heart in my home. She asked only a tiny amount of food and water each day, and the opportunity to be near and dear. Her loss still grieves me. I mourned as I have never mourned, for our closeness was unlike any I have ever known. Without words, she taught me love. Without action, she showed me the path of compassion. Through her eyes she said, "Without opening your door, you can open your heart to the world. Without looking out your window, you can see the essence of Life's Pathway."

I used to think my aunt had gone overboard in feelings for her dogs. She bred standard poodles and their care commanded the attention of her every waking moment. "Men are no damned good," she would say to me. As a sixteen year old, I did not understand her exclusivity with her pets. "I love my dogs," she said, as she trekked several miles a day into the mountains to tend the kennel she had built for them. Understandably, city ordinances would not allow her to keep the two dozen or so poodle dogs in her home. I felt sorry for her; I always suspected she had been disappointed in love.

My aunt, as an officer in the Women's Army Corps, had been sent overseas to establish USOs for the servicemen in the war effort. At the end of WWII—the battles in the European theater finished—her special companion and friend in Paris jubilantly announced he was anxious to return to his home *and his wife*. He left my aunt with the gift of a pet French poodle to remind her of their liaison in Paris in the military chaos of the 1940s. That great standard poodle, covered with chocolate curls, was my aunt's *avatar*. Some have remarked that a dog could never have been a fair exchange for a man in a woman's life. I'm not so sure. Why would she prefer a disloyal man, which her lover had been, to a dog that gave her unconditional love?

My aunt certainly had special rules for people and many for her dogs. She was a fierce anti-vivisectionist. In the 1940s, vivisection was the term used for experimenting, including surgical cutting, on live animals, particularly dogs. The battle between scientists and animal rights activists rages today and animals are still used for scientific experimentation. Animal rights activists continue to crusade to save them, even after sixty years of heated political battle.

Not many people could come up to my aunt's standards, but her dogs always met the challenge. I believe, having lost Kuan Yin, I can better understand my aunt's anguish. No doubt, her wonderful mother poodle communicated with her, talked about the wartime and what challenges a single woman army officer had to face. I am sure my aunt remembered with warmth the happy convivial days when her handsome officer romanced her. Every time she looked into her poodle's eyes, she remembered her youth, the freedom from the provincial town where she grew up. She remembered, too, that in Europe she was free to sing her beloved opera on stage in the Paris Opera Theatre.

I am also sure that she missed the lesson on compassion that her animal companion tried to teach her. Having given her passion to a dishonest man, she could not have compassion for him. Instead, she gave all her compassion to her poodles. Animals teach us in so many ways.

On reflection, I believe Kuan Yin's "Seven Selected Commandments for Pet Owners" should be expanded. As I cannot collaborate with her, I would like to add a few more to the list on my own:

VIII
Give Back the Love

Always feed and water your pet before you set your own table. A pet, like a little child, is totally dependent on you, and nurturing is the mistress or master's responsibility. Pets and small children cannot grab a snack or make a meal when you are preoccupied with your own interests. Don't let them wait for you to be in a good mood to take care of them.

IX

Cleanliness is Next to Godliness

Keep your pet clean. Clean the surroundings, pick up the papers, and clean up the droppings in the yard. Carry a Pooperscooper or a plastic bag when you walk the dog. It is not the neighbors' responsibility to do your job. I know people who regularly walk their dogs on the local high school's track and field. Imagine how the athletes feel when they tromp through droppings left by a pet belonging to a "taxpayer" who believes the track is his property. A dog cannot clean up after himself, but he does a great deal of cleaning up after human *baggage*: bad thoughts about real or imagined slights, which we carry around and foist carelessly upon others.

Curbing your dog and cleaning up after him shows the human's respect for himself, his animal companion, and others in the neighborhood. Humans can pat the dog and tell him what a good boy he is to have managed his "gift" in an appropriate way. If we expect the dog to act appropriately, we must also act appropriately. We must appreciate appropriate behavior and model it.

X
Protect the Innocent

Do not allow your pet to suffer. Never keep him unattended in the car in cold or hot weather. The same rule applies to your children. Helpless babies and animals have literally cooked in the heat of a closed car while the mistress, or mother, continued her shopping or the master dropped in for a brew on Friday afternoon. It is not unusual to read in the newspaper about an infant who froze to death in the back seat because the mother "forgot he was there."

It is a heinous act, in my opinion, to thoughtlessly put the big dog—that guards you—into the truck bed with no protection from harm. Kuan Yin and I saw a German shepherd literally bouncing around in the back of a pickup truck. After several miles of bumps and turns, the dog bounced from the truck bed into the traffic. The frantic owner gathered the dog's injured body and raced off to the vet for a painful recuperation from his shameful neglect.

What a brave dog to incarnate with that person. The dog's near-death experience was a wake-up call for this self-centered and insensitive human. Watching the dog undergo disbelief, confusion, and pain may have been the springboard to a more compassionate and aware human. Until that moment, the man seemed to have lived in a world of unbridled ego.

Those of us who witnessed this accident saw the overall Spirit Plan at work. Kuan Yin suspected that the person had been abusive all his life. With his shotgun racked in the cab of the truck, his wife timidly sitting by his side, and the dog stationed in back in the open truck bed, the driver had forged through life on his own terms. When he saw the dog sail through the air from his rear view mirror, he realized he had more lessons to learn. Kuan Yin conveyed to me that as the man knelt over the dog, she had locked her gaze into the man's eyes. He saw the shock, felt the trembling, and witnessed the dimming of the big dog's light. Kuan Yin whispered, "The German shepherd asked the man, 'Why?'" That's all it took.

Kuan Yin continued, "The German shepherd says that all his life, the burly man, now humbled, refused to open up and pay attention to life's lessons. He has always been rebellious and suspicious of others, overcompensating for his fears with bravado." I knew he would never forgive himself if the animal died. He would spend his all to make up for his gross negligence. Kuan Yin noted the bravery of the dog for choosing to enter such a man's life.

Those of us who witnessed the heartrending moment silently cried out to the man to change. The "No Fear" decal on the back of the truck referred to the shotgun and the powerful dog as symbols of the man's strength. With the dog broken and bleeding, the man called upon a greater strength to help him through his trial. Kuan Yin nuzzled my hand and said, with her soul, "It has taken a beautiful dog to change this man." Kuan Yin assured me that when the man realizes his mistake, he will admit it and will correct it. I dearly hoped that was true. I patted her and realized the message was not only for the man but also for all of us who witnessed the trauma.

XI
When Trauma Strikes, Act Responsibly

When trauma strikes, don't put your pet through heroic measures, saving his living *temporarily* only to extend his dying. Death may be a release while dying might be agonizingly painful.

The veterinarian in the emergency room called me every two hours during that turbulent night. That horrible windy night! At 8 p.m., he called to say Kuan Yin had suffered two more neurological episodes or seizures—he wasn't sure—in front of his eyes, so he administered Valium. At 10 p.m., he called to tell me she was sleeping peacefully and hoped the neurologist could help in the morning. At midnight, he called to say the lab tests had come back from nearby Porter Hospital. The report didn't look good.

While the blood tests should have shown 200,000 to 500,000 platelets, Kuan Yin's count was only 2,000. It looked as though her immune system had crashed. In the meantime, he had re-examined her body and found small bruises. Concerned that she had been experiencing repeated hemorrhaging, he had given her Valium rectally, which should have kept her at peace through the night.

At 3:45 a.m., he called again to say that Kuan Yin had just experienced two more massive episodes of violent shaking and racing feet. Her pupils had closed to pinpoints, yet because her eyes were open during the seizure or convulsion, the veterinarian was not sure which to call it. Each time he telephoned, I awakened, startled, from troubled sleep. Each time he made his report and hung up, I cried violently. I saw my loss clearly before me. I could not imagine reversal of her trauma, and I could not bear to put her through more pain. When the doctor called for the last time, I begged him to stop her episodes and release her from her pain. Actually, he had already given her Pentathol because the Valium had not done its job. I literally begged him to increase the dosage and assist her to her peace. On his own, he had already made that decision. I could faintly hear Kuan Yin calling, "Mistress will gain true mastery by letting things go their own way. Nothing can be gained by interfering."

XII
Remember to Play and to Pray

I had always realized that, throughout her life with me, Kuan Yin was bringing me a sense of play and great comfort. I had tried to return that joy and comfort to her each day as I loved her unconditionally. She taught me that love has no limits and that great satisfaction exists in extending oneself to service without expectations attached. Connecting with me, she would say, "Mistress possesses nothing. The more she does for others, the happier she is. The more she gives to others, the wealthier she is."

I felt rich when, searching for her gummy bone, I delighted her. She pranced around me and teased me, egging me on to let me know if my search was "hot" or "cold." I disregarded how ridiculous I must look crawling around on the carpet—haunch over head—peeking under chairs and sofa, peering into corners, looking for the lost toy. Kuan Yin barked approval. She always showed approval with an upturned look, a tiny lick on the hand, or a playful bark.

I noticed that same reaction when I observed men and their dogs out playing Frisbee on the green belt. Men threw the disks; the dogs retrieved them. If a man hesitated too long, the dog nudged him or barked encouragingly, waiting patiently for the man to get the message. Animal companions enjoy the play as much as their humans do. Kittens love to bat at a ball of string, pounce on a toy mouse, or leap from table to ledge and back again playing "Great Hunter." Play is healthy. It is a conscious abandonment of routine and regimen. Filled with laughter and surprise, play is activity for the sheer pleasure of the moment. Animal companions teach humans that play is fun and play is necessary.

Prayer is also necessary. In whatever form, to whatever benevolent Essence, prayer brings attention to the center. Kuan Yin was right to call a hospital a "house of prayer." Trust in the doctor requires an act of faith—and a mistress, like a parent, must pray to make the right decisions in the end. She must also pray to be worthy of such unconditional love—and the continued affection and comfort a loving pet brings.

The prayers in the hospital should be those of praise and thanksgiving for the years or days of joy one's pet can bring. Kuan Yin gave me more than twelve hundred days of happiness and comfort. I remember how her birthday gave me the opportunity to invite an octogenarian and a nonagenarian into my home for a party. The latter, Susan, who still lived by herself successfully, had brought Kuan Yin a tiny Bronco shirt, which became the center of attraction for the group and springboard for laughter for all. Susan and Doris celebrated Kuan Yin's first birthday luncheon as if she were a favored child. She *was* a

The Birthday Party

*. . . her birthday gave me the opportunity to invite an octogenarian
and a nonagenarian into my home for a party.*

favored child…mine. Once, one of my grown sons jokingly asked me, "Mom, when I die, can I come back as your dog?" He did not remember that when *he* was a child, I had treated no one better than I treated him. Perhaps as he noticed my connection with Kuan Yin, he became aware of a softness that was separated from the training part of a mother's role. Youngsters may forget the cuddles of childhood and remember only the constraints they felt as rebellious teens. Conflict often masks the calm.

Live and Love Each Precious Day

I had traveled hundreds of miles in a windstorm to receive Kuan Yin in my arms when she was a puppy. Nearly four years later, she left in the wake of the Hale-Bopp comet, cold weather, and more severe wind. At each moment, I felt the force of nature dramatically changing my life. I was alone again. It was up to me to learn from the lessons Kuan Yin taught in our quiet moments. She taught me I did not have to be powerful to be successful; I did not have to wear a dress suit with hose and heels to maintain prestige. She taught me the loneliest people in the community need to be invited to a party. They would provide the entertainment when the party got dull. Having retired from a career of forty years, I learned I did not have to fear aging. She taught me the greatest revelation of all: *I no longer had to act like Wonder Woman to be considered wonderful.*

Kuan Yin said in her thoughts, "Mistress must give up herself to whatever the moment brings. She knows one day she will die. Hold nothing back from life; therefore be ready for death as a man is ready for sleep after a good day's work." Because of her teaching, I realize that each separate being in the universe returns to the common Source. Returning to the Source is serenity.

As I walk through the markets and the pathways past the dogs walking their owners, I see in their eyes the wisdom of Kuan Yin and I am sadly glad. I am glad that Kuan Yin forced me out of my shell and made me walk in the sunlight each day. I am glad she exercised me by playing ball and making me look under the couch for her gummy bone. I am glad she introduced me to so many wonderful pets and their people who became Kuan Yin's friends. And I am glad she and I had *many* nonsense parties and serious conversations my friends would never understand.

She was Kuan Yin, and she was, indeed, adorable.

Tail of the Tale

When Kuan Yin was so ill, I was frustrated that her veterinarian was out of town and I could not get answers about her illness. Days before the seizures began, I had called in desperation to the Department of Veterinary Medicine at Colorado State University in Fort Collins, Colorado, to make an appointment. Doctors at the school were to have run tests and given her a thorough examination to evaluate why she was pronounced well after the surgery yet could not stand on all four legs. I do not know if specialists could have prevented what happened.

On the very night before our appointment at the School of Veterinary Medicine, she had her seizures. At pre-dawn, on the day of our scheduled appointment with the specialists there, Kuan Yin made her Transition.

I do not know if just a few hours would have made a difference. The veterinarian at the emergency hospital told me that her ailment stemmed from rash in-breeding practiced at a puppy mill. People who want to make a quick dollar indiscriminately breed a sire with his heir, the bitch with hers. The consequence of that kind of inbreeding can cause grave medical problems for the dog, huge medical expenses for the owner, and pain and agony of loss of the pet. The title of the disorder that caused her death was an unpronounceable word, which simply means "unknown." That vague word made her passing even worse as I continued to ask the question, "Why?"

When Kuan Yin died, my call to cancel the appointment elicited a great deal of care and concern from the staff there. A grief counselor promptly called me and spent a long time talking with me. The counselor perceived the depth of my grief. She told me Kuan Yin's loss had become the symbol of *all* the unmourned losses I had experienced in the past. I thought about that and realized I had never truly grieved before. My parents had been in a distant part of the country when they passed away. My mother's death, just two years before, had caused an explosion of unspoken resentments between siblings. The turmoil after her death denied me the opportunity to mourn with my sister, with whom I had been estranged emotionally for decades. Instead of resolving our perceived differences and petty jealousies, we reverted to the childish actions of dumping and blaming, so prevalent in our youth.

Finally, after a marriage of two decades that produced three sons, I got a divorce without resolving it with my family. I had never vocalized my pain to my grown children. They had always seen me as a self-contained, strong woman who undoubtedly had initiated the divorce because of some "Woman's Lib" ethic. How could I discuss the intimate reasons that culminated in pain for all the family? Explaining the divorce to boys who could identify only with their father's point of view would have sounded like casting blame. As an educator, I had seen parents tear up their children by scandalizing each other. Still, I could not bring myself to discuss the details even to adult children. Consequently, they held resentments for years after the divorce. They simply withdrew emotionally from me.

The decision to divorce hurt, but the withholding of affection and loyalty from my family hurt ever so much more. We never talked about it. In a way, it was like Kuan Yin's leaving for no foreseeable reason. For nearly two decades, I had closed up the grief within and kept a pleasant countenance to shield my family from the unspoken disappointment and emotional distancing that ended my marriage.

I had never mourned other unresolved issues. Retirement came long before I had planned to leave my beloved profession. Early retirement was, for me, a condemnation to old age. I was not ready to give up the daily active life, the responsibility, and the pleasure of helping mold the lives of young people. In a way, that also was like losing my sons to the divorce. My soul was, indeed, in turmoil.

The sorrow of my mother's passing was really grief for a relationship that had never existed. The pain of my sister's unresolved anger and resentment of me was relieved only by distance. The sadness and regret for my failed marriage began long before the divorce, as unspoken concerns welled deep within. I felt I had been cast adrift. By contrast, Kuan Yin had shown me more affection, more loyalty, and more unconditional love than I had ever known before. Kuan Yin had filled a void.

Now that she was gone, I swirled in a sea of disbelief and anger and was overcome by a deep sense of depression and guilt. "What did I do wrong?" I asked the universe. Perhaps I had dropped a pill that she picked up, thinking it was a crust of something wonderful. Maybe she got lead poisoning from the wicker chair that she sometimes chewed. Who knows? I speculated endlessly to no avail.

I continued to search for answers about all my losses. I longed to know why I never experienced a warm mother-daughter relationship. When she was in her seventies, I remember my mother once saying, "Looking back, I realize I never knew you girls." I agonized over the question of why she didn't get to know me. I questioned why my sister and I had never grown close as children and why—as adults—we had never resolved childhood animosities. Getting to the core of the matter, I asked why they occurred in the first place. Yet mostly I was tormented with the recurring question, "Why, oh why, did my marriage of twenty-one years fade and die with no concrete villain?"

People (like me) who transfer all their love to their pets feel entrapped when they lose their loving dog or cat. They live in a box canyon that has only one way out. Sheltered from the real world in a Communion of Silent Love with the animal, bereaved owners must now face the real challenge of relating to people again. They must leave the dark chasm of internal misery and head out into the light once again. Life must go on, for the only constant in life is change.

Kuan Yin would say, "Mistress must use her own light and return to the Source of Light. This is called Practicing Eternity."

"How can I do this, when I am so unhappy?" I might ask, and I know she would answer, "By looking inside yourself."

One way to begin is through grief counseling, which is available in most major cities. In its "Changes Program," Colorado State University provides grief counseling to people who have lost their pets. Their telephone call definitely helped me at a time when I lived alone and did not know where to turn. My friends had all listened quietly and offered their condolences. They knew how much I had loved the little Maltese; however, there was a limit to how long they could continue listening and consoling. I knew I needed to get a grip on the reality that Kuan Yin was gone.

Instead of getting counseling, however, I simply hung on to my grief as if it were the only remaining fragment of a pleasant life. I did everything except wear black, the "widow's weeds," that tell the world one is in mourning. My face showed the sorrow I felt, and eventually my body language reflected my grief. Just as with the relationship problems I had with my birth family and my former husband, instead of getting help, I continued to grieve in silence and tuck the pain deep within. The remembrance of my loss gnawed at me for years. I had to force myself to remain strong. Cicero has said that the cure for grief is action, but I found that action alone only delayed the cure.

At the time of my divorce, I was working in the public schools. I chose not to accept the grief services available there. I used every excuse to keep from facing the problem. I was "too busy." I had my classes to plan, numerous visitations to make, then grades to calculate. I had plants to water (there was *something* in my life left to care for, after all) and I always had my nails to file. Previously, I had tried group counseling for my dysfunctional family problems, but came away from them feeling that this experience was like the blind leading the blind. "What shall we talk about now?" the facilitator might say. I felt it wasted my time, and I was embarrassed to share my pain and my guilt with other members of the group who worked with me.

Like a tortoise, I pulled my head into my shell and harbored my grief. I had written the first several chapters of this book—the humorous side—when Kuan Yin was living with me. After she left, I could not find enough humor within myself to continue the remaining planned chapters. Kuan Yin was not there to help me see the bright side. I could no longer write the funny perspective of the little dog with the goddess name. I was stuck.

Three years after her death, I joined a publishing group. I located an editor to start the process of publishing my shortened book of humor. I tried to explain my goals to her. I choked as I spoke of the book. On our first meeting, when I mentioned the beloved dog's name, tears trickled down my cheeks. Embarrassed by my emotions, I excused myself with the promise to continue the discussion later. I asked myself, "How on earth will I ever be able to sell a book I cannot talk about?"

I went home and wrote the chapter I now call, "The Tail of the Tale." I needed to express my pain. Slowly, I uncovered the problem. Layer by layer, I peeled away the sorrows and exposed the boils around my soul. Thinking about my feelings was painful. My emotional side had always been an embarrassment to me, for as a youngster I was taught that showing emotional pain was a sign of weakness or willfulness.

Still, my editor urged me on. Writing about my feelings also hurt, but it seemed to bring a sense of release. As I discussed the problem of grief, I revisited the grief packet

CSU had sent me years before. I talked to a grief counselor there and explained how I had felt when I lost my pet. The more I discussed my feelings with this trained professional, the more I was able to speak calmly about them. As the editor sent corrections to the manuscript, I was forced to discuss word choice and goals. I began to treat the subject of loss more objectively.

As people who write journals know, writing about problems lessens their power. I still hated the pain, but acknowledging it and honoring it, vocalizing and writing about it helped me recognize the sources of the unending hurt I had felt for so many years of my life. By ignoring the aching pain, I had allowed it to grow. By stuffing it in the dark closet of my heart, I was shutting out the joy that still abounds in the light of day.

Slowly, as the bruised outer petals fell away, a soft center began to emerge. Kuan Yin had given me a reason to talk about my feelings. She expressed love for me, and I was free to express my love to her. Humans communicate with their animal companions by touch and by talking softly and enthusiastically to them. I realized that is also how humans must communicate with each other. The problem lies in finding another human who freely communicates in the same loving way.

Kuan Yin was a sublime substitute for lost loves. When others hurt me, I simply shut them out—all of them, including friends and family. I know Kuan Yin would say something like, "Mistress must be patient with both friends and enemies. Think of enemies as shadows you cast yourself." For decades, I had ignored the issues, expecting them to fall away. I had wrapped all my pent-up affections around Kuan Yin's small being. When she died, her fragile body epitomized my fragile soul. When she died, a little of my own soul went with her.

As the chapters in the book turned to grief and the healing process, and as I uncovered more resources, I slowly began to heal my psychic pain. Kuan Yin would say, "Accomplish the great task by a series of small acts. Mistress must confront the difficult while it is still easy." Talking to other bereaved pet owners, I saw that they also felt getting over their grief was painful and time-consuming. I continued the process. I read many self-help books and talked to many people about their own losses. I allowed the tears to flow freely. Eventually they dried up. Well, most of them. When we bring pets into our lives, we forget that their life spans are far shorter than ours. Many people told me of their experiences with four or five beloved pets whom they loved or lost. Loving and losing is painful even if the realities are rational. Losing a love does not make one rational.

Eventually, I opened my life to new connections. I began to talk to pet owners in the malls and in the markets again. I often stooped down to pet a little white dog and get a "puppy fix." I told people about Kuan Yin and felt the compassion in their faces. I explained to the dentist why I had not brought my pet taxi into the office when I had a dental treatment. I talked to the boy at the grocery checkout stand and told him why the pet taxi was not at the bottom of the shopping basket as it had been for years.

As the book emerged, I met and married a wonderful man. He had lost his wife and—through her long illness—his business. I was stunned to discover, as I was moving into his house, that he had a white porcelain statue the same size and pose as the one I had

In the Driver's Seat

*. . . side by side in a moving automobile — Filio sitting tall and imposing on the passenger's side.
It caused a great deal of curiosity from passersby.*

brought to the marriage. It was the standing, benevolent goddess Kuan Yin, which his parents had brought from China when they were missionaries. I was also amazed how affectionate my husband was to his pet Airedale and how that curly-haired dog showed an immediate affinity for me. He looked nothing like Kuan Yin, but when I gazed into his eyes, we somehow connected. I perceived a softness about my husband whenever he talked about how Filio came into his life "just in the nick of time." He spoke of Filio as if he were a beloved brother, told about their adventures, and laughed when others looked twice at the two of them side by side in a moving automobile—Filio sitting tall and imposing on the passenger's side. It caused a great deal of curiosity from passersby.

Before my Kuan Yin died, I had been completely unaware that schools of Veterinary Medicine provide counseling services. I did not know that some schools even provide web sites, grief support programs, pet loss support, and even a pet loss hotline. Some also provide grief education classes and—best of all—many of their services are free.

If you would like to contact a reassuring voice, I suggest you call your local university's department of veterinary medicine and/or refer to the resources provided in the next chapter. To the people at CSU, who delivered the kindnesses and information I sorely needed, I am grateful. They and their colleagues are Kuan Yin's legacy.

Good Grief

Grief is a healthy psychological response to the loss of a treasured loved one. It is a normal and unavoidable reaction to experiencing deep, painful, and difficult feelings. To some, the loss of a pet can be as traumatic as the loss of a human who is close. To others, that loss can be more so. In many cases, people who live alone often form close relationships with their pets while they alienate themselves from human contact. The pet takes on virtues humans seldom achieve, including unconditional love, loyalty, constant presence, and reliable companionship. The loss of such a pet leaves a big hole in daily life, often bringing on a deeper sense of isolation. Grief is the price one pays for the joy of unconditional love.

Sometimes, the loss of a pet symbolizes unresolved losses of other kinds. Memories of the death of parents, spouses, or children may spring from the past and embed themselves in the death of a pet. Thoughts of lost opportunities, divorce, forced retirement, or a lost job are triggered by the void left by the loving pet—meant to take the place of the departed loved ones or lost opportunities. When experiencing the process is denied, grief grows stronger and seeks all available avenues to be resolved, like a river without an outlet.

Grief has no time schedule. One who grieves must take time to understand the loss and fill the void that exists where a friend once stood. If you are grieving, honor your feelings. Express your pain, acknowledge your loss, and seek ways to heal without worrying what others will think. Time heals, but "time takes time." If you try to hurry the process or suppress your feelings, you may actually prolong the healing timetable.

Further, experiencing death of another being brings us face to face with our own mortality. When my last parent died, I realized I was indeed the "older generation" in my family. That was a sobering thought. Perhaps grief expresses our subconscious sadness about our own passing when we do not understand or accept death's sanctity.

Grief takes on many forms. I experienced a combination of those forms I faced the empty rooms where once there was activity of abounding joy.

Physically, I felt exhausted from crying and, intellectually, I was embarrassed that tears appeared at the slightest mention of Kuan Yin. Most of the time, I could not speak to my friends about her death without breaking down. That emotional reaction lasted for three years and occasionally still pops up when I least expect it.

The fascination and foreboding of death was overwhelming to me because I had not come to grips with mortality. I couldn't get my mind off Kuan Yin's passing. She had become such an integral part of my daily life; I had to reprogram my activities. Going grocery shopping, visiting the dentist, having my hair or nails done reminded me constantly I was alone. People at the grocery store, the dentist, and the beautician were used to seeing me carry the pet taxi and park it while my hands were busy. They made a point to ask me, "Where is she? What happened to her? How could that happen to such a young dog?" I could barely speak. Many empathized and told me about their own loss of a pet. Some expressed deep pain and some were quite matter-of-fact. All admitted hurting.

All in all, I felt sorry for myself. I was angry with the farm family who bred dogs indiscriminately and sold them as fast as they could. I had planned to have my precious pet with me for at least a decade, maybe fifteen years. I was sure, with the good care I gave her, Kuan Yin would join me well into my old age. "Why me?" I asked the universe. "Why now, when I was so happy?"

I tried to keep busy. As usual, I threw myself into my work at the university. I took on more responsibility, volunteered to work with students in the far reaches of metropolitan Denver. I even took assignments in adjacent counties, requiring long drives of two hours or more. I did my shopping long after I finished work because I had no reason to go home. By distracting my mind from the issue of death, I simply extended the time it would take to resolve my feelings.

I never thought God had caused my loss. God's greatness and all-encompassing goodness does not cause misfortune. But I had no answers. Not even the veterinarians could explain the reason for her death. The fact that there was no one to blame left me frustrated and totally bewildered. Kuan Yin would say that the path into the light seems dark. "If you blame someone else, there is no end to blame."

The unfairness of knowing she was not yet even four years old made the loss even more difficult. It also made me think of all my other losses. I was looking for someone or something to blame, and I realized that was a useless act. "Mistress must remain serene in the midst of sorrow," I could feel her saying. "Therefore, evil cannot enter your heart." I knew she was right when she said, "Mistress must fulfill her own obligations and correct her own mistakes. She must do what she needs to do and demand nothing of others." I pondered the wasted energy I had spent looking for reasons, and I knew I simply had to move on.

How could a person become so attached to an animal when she was never attached to a human in the same way? Perhaps the memory of loss—like the WWII captain who left my aunt in Paris to return to his wife when the war ended—was constantly rekindled. Each time one of my aunt's French poodles died, the loss of a promised marriage returned to her. At last, I could relate to her attachment to her dogs. The errant captain had given her the first French poodle puppy as a going-away present.

Scores of memories flowed into my mind as Kuan Yin's death brought a halt to my comfortable new life of companionship. I saw Kuan Yin's coming as a wonderful transition from the excitement of the daily work world to the quiet life of research, contemplation, and writing. At work, there was never a time when scores of people did not flow in and out of my office with problems to solve. I never pined away for the scores of people, but working out of my home, I had no one with whom I could talk. Talking—negotiating, mediating, and problem-solving in a group—had always been a big part of my life. I realized I was in trouble when my closest friends were the mechanic who repaired my car, the postman who brought the bills, the hairdresser who caught me up on the recent action at the film festival, and the green grocer who told me about out of season fruits or vegetables flown in from Argentina. Kuan Yin had saved me from the illusion that friendly acquaintances were true friends.

Before her coming, my work had rescued me from the losses I had experienced after divorce—life as a cooperating unit, status as a wife and mother—role losses I had not mourned. Work, thank goodness, kept me from socializing and seeking out a new spouse—avoiding the mistake of a rebound relationship and the problems it can bring. Yes, I had avoided the deep, disturbing feelings that flashed momentarily in my memories. Yet, I had really postponed them, letting them stockpile in the dark cave of my subconscious. Kuan Yin saved me from the illusion that if I buried myself in work, all my unresolved issues would vanish. She once said, "Mistress knows *that* behavior is for ostriches."

Retirement also exposed layers of losses. So, Kuan Yin's presence was comfortable; she did not intrude on my thoughts, yet she seemed to understand that I really wanted a good listener. What I *didn't* want were probing questions about my childhood, my marriage, the glass ceiling. They were too painful to answer. Anyway, Kuan Yin was not interested in the details of a dysfunctional family, a collapsing marriage, or an inner-circle network of exclusion.

By her very dog nature, she took on a personality. I talked to her as if she were a child, a companion, and a colleague. I communicated with her in my thoughts. She responded as if she understood. She did not interfere with my schedule; I merely included her in everything I did. She had no agenda; only *her* needs motivated my decisions. And her needs always came first. Her food, water, hygiene, and health were my priorities. Nothing was too good or too much trouble to give her. I treated her as I had treated my own children when they were tots.

One does not forget how to nurture. It's like riding a bicycle, I guess. It all comes back. The nurturer in my personality stepped out of the shadows and illuminated the room. Kuan Yin's presence reflected the light and gave me peace. Her listening felt like good therapy.

I have said that I had experienced multiple losses in my birth family and losses of relationships among my own family members, who I felt had abandoned me after the divorce. Somehow I believed I could have prevented those losses and had taken on responsibility for them.

Because Kuan Yin was a young dog, her loss was unexpected in spite of the appearance of complications after her surgery. Again, I took responsibility for having done something wrong in my care for her. I felt guilty that I was not present at her death, nor could I bear to view her body afterwards. I remembered over and over watching her wobble down the hallway after her knees had healed. I puzzled over her appearance of being lost, confused, or blind when she wandered beneath the chair legs. All this made my healing more difficult. I had to give up guilt. I had to quit blaming myself. Kuan Yin would say, "Mistress must see things as they are without trying to control them. She must let them go their own way and reside in the center of the circle." I needed to seek my own center and detach from the losses with love and compassion. I had to learn to let go.

Pain is a life-saving warning that something is terribly wrong. Once, I experienced overwhelming pain in nearly every part of my body. It forced me to go to the doctor, take exploratory tests, and undergo other procedures I would have just dismissed except the pain was more than I could bear. An MRI revealed a grapefruit-sized cyst growing on a long stem from one of my ovaries. The unruly growth was twisting on its stem as it bashed into nerves along the spine. This pain was a harbinger of a possible misfortune, for when the surgeon opened it up to take a biopsy, she discovered it was full of gangrene. More procrastinating and Wonder Woman attitudes would have left a roomful of mourning heirs wondering what had happened.

Grief is psychic pain. It is a messenger sent to let us know what we had is gone. Grief tells us we are human, we need others, and we suffer when our friends, loved ones, or support systems are gone. If we pay attention to it, we can grow from every grief experience.

When Kuan Yin did not show appropriate recovery from her knee surgery, I began to worry about "what if." When she ran down the hall to meet me in a valiant burst of energy, only to fall into a seizure at my feet, I anticipated her loss. I could not envision a reversal of the symptoms I had been carefully watching. As she lay cushioned on a deep-pile sheepskin in the emergency room, she experienced more episodes of seizure. Each time the veterinarian telephoned me, I became more convinced she was losing the battle. I thought of how badly it felt to lose her, but more importantly, I thought how selfish it would be to prolong her suffering by grasping at impossibilities.

Near the end, when she was not responding to medication, I could stand her pain no longer. I begged the veterinarian to release her from the existence she was enduring. I did not hesitate; I knew it was my decision to take responsible action.

I had said my final good-bye while she was curled in my lap in the emergency room. She lay very still as I stroked her beautiful long, white fur. She had recently visited the groomer who had cleaned her up after the surgery—a ball of fluffy white, the essence of pure beauty. She did not lift her face to look at me with her round, jellybean eyes. She did not cock her head to hear me more clearly. I could see she was, indeed, going on a different pathway and a different journey from mine. I had held her and stroked her for nearly an hour when the attendant came in to take her to the hospital observation kennel. As he scooped her up tenderly and left the room, I knew I had seen Kuan Yin for the last time.

I did not want to see her in death, for I knew her spirit would no longer be with her body. Her spirit was exactly what I had loved; it would soon be in a better place than the observation kennel in a hospital. Kuan Yin would leave me with this lesson, "The way to use life is to *do* everything through *being*."

Kuan Yin's memorial is neither a marker nor a stone. It is the loving memory emblazoned in my heart.

Journey of the Red Balloon

After all the reading and all the conversing with the experts, at last it came time to go deep within my heart and soul and make the brave attempt to say the final goodbye. For four years, I had steadfastly refused to let go of Kuan Yin and move forward. I have friends who have kept the ashes of their dogs in a jar on the dresser, the ashes of a husband on a shelf in the closet. Clinging to the ashen remains, they refused to accept reality and put the issue at rest. I sincerely feel that hoarding those ashes keeps the illusion of life alive. It keeps the dead from a final resting place and the living in a listless dream state. It also maintains a space of power that sets up a barricade to the doors of a heart that cannot fully accept others in its place. Owners cannot bring themselves to bring another animal companion into their lives because they believe they cannot ever replace the beloved pet. Those who keep ashes of spouses shut out a new possibility because the reminder is always there for the prospective new partner.

Just as we bury the body, it is much better to return the ashes to the universe. Hanging on to grief is a prolonged painful experience, an unhealthy experience. In a way, holding on is a form of denial that the loved one is truly gone. I have said the word *gone* when what I need to say is the word *dead*. Death and all its connecting words are anathema in American society. Death is a condition I greatly feared. I contemplated what I must do to move beyond grief and into growth.

Early in the 1980s, I had purchased a tape from a religious center. I have since forgotten the title and no longer have the tape, but the theme of the powerful self-help technique has remained with me for over twenty years. The self-hypnotic technique is called *The Red Balloon*. That technique is used by psychologists and healers to bring closure to dead issues, relationships, loved ones, and animal companions. It is a means of visualizing what we are afraid to face: the transition from this life into the unknown afterlife.

When I made the commitment to heal, I was ready to face reality by employing this wonderful technique. It helped me and it has helped others whom I love. I share this experience with you with the understanding that it is not of my own creation. If you care to try it, here is what you must do:

Close your eyes and breathe deeply. Inhale the air as far as it will go, filling your lungs completely. Now exhale it as thoroughly as possible. Continue this deep breathing for several breaths. Notice how the air fills your lungs fully and notice how it feels when you expel it so completely that there is not even a wisp of air inside your lungs. Just breathe. Listen to sounds of the air filling and emptying your lungs. Air is necessary to life. Allow the life-giving air to fill your lungs completely and know that you are living fully in the moment.

Think of a beautiful place in the world, one where you have felt safe and happy. Perhaps it is on a mountaintop with snowy ice caps all within near view. Perhaps it is on the shore of sunny California or a remote island in the Pacific. Choose a truly wonderful place: a dense forest, a lush jungle, a placid desert, or the vast plains with wheat ripening near the harvest. Be comfortable as you visualize this happy place of your choosing.

Visualize a beautiful, red, hot air balloon just down the path from you. Picture yourself accompanying your lost loved one to the balloon's lovely basket still resting softly on the ground. Open the basket's gate and gently help your loved one inside. Close the gate securely. Step back as you see the balloon begin to rise off the ground slowly and gracefully. Picture your loved one looking over the edge of the balloon's basket, safe and sound and looking happy to be going on the wonderful journey ahead. Breathe deeply several times.

As the balloon rises, you may need to apologize for acts of omission and neglect or for some slight you may have caused your loved one. Sincere apology is necessary to send your beloved on the journey. Ask also for forgiveness and send your own forgiveness to your loved one if that is appropriate. Talk it over. Make peace with your friend and wave thoughtfully. Send your thanks and appreciation. Smile warmly and tell the beloved of the joy you felt in your journey together on this earth. Listen. Listen to the cadence of your own breath, your own voice, and the swishing sound of the hot air filling the balloon. Listen to the passing of time. Breathe deeply. Hear your own breath of life and the swishing sound of the balloon as the air heats making the balloon rise.

Watch how the balloon rises higher and higher on this beautiful day. See the image of the balloon against the bright blue, cloudless sky. As it rises into the atmosphere, hum or sing softly some tune you both have loved. Keep your eye on the vanishing pinpoint of red and when it is gone from sight, take a deep breath and say, "Good-bye, I have loved you."

You may need to do this exercise once, or you may need to repeat it several evenings over time before you go to sleep. Expect to cry. Allow the tears, the sobs, to come freely. Hold nothing back. Give your emotions full sway and allow yourself to feel the pain, and when it comes, allow yourself to experience release. This is *catharsis.* Celebrate your feelings and accept release.

Allow your beloved also to experience that release. Your dead issue, your failed relationship, your marriage, your parenting, your loving of the past is now out of sight, gone from your life. Be still, and allow the transition from the here and now to the welcoming universe. Do not selfishly hang on. Let go. Detach with love.

Concentrating now on your breathing again, allow yourself to return to the present reality. Feel a lighter heart, a cleaner soul. Open your eyes and when you are ready, go to sleep or rest. You need peaceful moments and a long private time of reflection. You may simply cry yourself to sleep.

When you have sent your beloved safely on the new journey, know that you are also safely on yours. As time passes, you must re-enter the mainstream of life and become part of the flow of time. You have forgiven and been forgiven. Now is time to move on and to celebrate Life. Prepare yourself for the journey ahead.

The Red Balloon

*When you have sent your beloved safely on the new journey,
know that you are also safely on yours.*

Posthumous Tribute

Late in the process of writing *Maltese Crossing*, I discovered that Dr. Shelby Lewis Walch was the architect of the Red Balloon concept. Hours of researching the Denver Public Library and the medical libraries of Colorado University and Colorado State University—as well as the Library of Congress, the United States Copyright Office sources, Patent Office databases, and other international resources on the Internet—produced hundreds of businesses that used the words *red* and *balloon* in their titles. Only one reference produced the name of the individual who developed the Red Balloon process. On the Internet, the "Social Security Death Index Search"[1] results produced a social security number, which allowed me to further research Dr. Walch's employment at the Hospital from which he retired in 1972. Continuing the research, I located the *Directory of the American Psychological Association, 1997 Edition*. In it I found the particulars of his leadership as assistant clinical psychologist and Project Director in the Department of Child Health Division at Metropolitan State Hospital.

---

[1] Geneaology.com, LLC, "Social Security Death Index Search Results."

A graduate of the University of Texas with specialties in hypnotherapy and psychotherapy, Dr. Walch developed the concept of the Red Balloon when he worked at Metropolitan State Hospital in Norwalk, California. His article, "The Red Balloon Technique of Hypnotherapy: A Clinical Note," appeared in a 1976 issue of *The International Journal of Clinical and Experimental Hypnosis, Vol. XXIV,* No. 1, pp. 10-12. The concept of visualizing oneself in the act of attaching a container of problems, losses, and lost individuals to a balloon that would sail to infinity—perhaps to a better place—helped to finalize the issues that people clung to and release the guilt that made them sick. From the anguish of physical and emotional pain, the red balloon moves one's spirit upward because that is the only direction left to go.

In his article, Dr. Walch stated that many of his colleagues had also used the technique to great relief of their patients. Twenty-three years ago, when I first heard a tape that mentioned the concept, I internalized the idea and used it whenever I needed to let go.[2] Subsequently, I have also used it with family and friends to help alleviate their burdens. In this book, I have suggested its use to help sorrowing humans release their beloved deceased companion and move forward, in the hope of finding another and beginning a new loving relationship. Although grief is the price we pay for the loss of unconditional love, growth through grief proves we are decent humans capable of living joyfully and loving deeply.

---

[2] The tape I remembered did not use the container into which to put the objects and attach it to the balloon. My use of the concept used only a hot air balloon because I had no knowledge of the container and had not read Dr. Walch's study.

I gratefully attribute credit and appreciation to Dr. Walch, the hypnotherapist whose idea helped his patients accept the finality of death and guilt issues and create new realities for themselves. And I ascribe thankful tribute posthumously to a brilliant mind. Born September 23, 1925, Dr. Walch died in Honolulu, Hawaii, August, 1984.

— *P.D. Sargent,* 2002

Resources

Nothing can really replace your lost pet, but you may take some comfort in connecting with others who have shared the same experience. This Resources section provides you with names of search engines and web sites of up-to-date addresses and telephone numbers for local counseling, support services, and body cemeteries. These web sites also list national support hotlines and organizations, and web site and Internet support services. Finally, this section includes a reading list concerning loss, death, grief and the healing process. It is helpful to identify with the experiences of others and discuss how they got through the pain.

My own experience with the School of Veterinary Medicine at Colorado State University (CSU) leads me to believe that schools of Veterinary Medicine are the first line of help. I urge you to contact one in or near your state or province. CSU's Change Program is on the web at the following address: http://www.cumbs.coloradostate.edu/changes/

Note: for those who do not have home Internet access, call your local library for assistance.

Universities with Schools of Veterinary Medicine

As of this writing, thirty-one Colleges of Veterinary Medicine serve North America. In addition to education in the field of veterinary medicine, they also provide research and specialized health care to animals. Many professionals on staff counsel patrons at the time of pet loss. A current list of accredited veterinary schools is located at the following address: http://www.avma.org/careforanimals/animatedjourneys/aboutvets/vetschools.asp

You may also contact the American Veterinary Medical Association at this web site: http://www.avma.org/care4pets/lossandi.htm

National Resources Hotlines

A list of hotlines is at: http://www.avma.org/care4pets/aumaloss.htar

Association for Pet Loss and Bereavement
P.O. Box 106
Brooklyn, NY 11230
http://www.aplb.org   718-382-0690

American Society for the Prevention of Cruelty to Animals
424 East 92 Street
New York, NY 10128-6804
National Pet Loss Hotline   212-876-7700 ext. 4355
http://www.aspca.org/site/PageServer?pagename=animed_pets_petloss

Web Site Support Services

America Online: Support groups can be found at Keyword: Pet Care, under Animals in Society.

Association for Pet Loss and Bereavement
P.O. Box 106 , Brooklyn, NY 11230
http://www.aplb.org   718-382-0690

American Veterinary Medical Association:
See this Web site for list of veterinary medicine schools including grief counseling services.
http://www.avma.org/care4pets/lossandi.htm

Marty Tousley:
http://www.griefhealing.com/petlinks.htm

Pet Loss and Grief Support:
http://www.creatures.com/petloss.htm

Pet Loss Resources:
http://www.superdog.com/petloss.htm
http://thunder.prohosting.com/~easyshop

Pet Loss Memorials and Tributes:
http://www.foreverpets.com/petloss.htm

Pet Loss Support, Rainbow Bridge, Candle Ceremony:
http://www.rainbowsbridge.com

Pet Memorials:
http://www.animalnews.com/memorial/

Rainbow Bridge:
http://www.rainbowsbridge.com

Further Reading on Loss, Death, and Grief

Children, Loss, and Grief

Brackenridge, S. *Because of Flowers and Dancers*. Veterinary Practice Publishing Company, 1996.

Brown, M. *The Dead Bird*. Harper Junior, New edition, William Morrow and Co., 2002.

Buscaglia, L. *The Fall of Freddie the Leaf: A Story for All Ages.* Holt, Rinehart, and & Winston, 1983.

Carrick, C. *The Accident*. Houghton Mifflin Co., 1981 O.P.

Dahm, Paul C. *The Rainbow Bridge*. Running Tide Press, 1997.

Davis, C. *For Every Dog an Angel: The Forever Dog.* Lighthearted Press, 1997.

Gipson, F. *Old Yeller*. HarperCollins, 1956. Reprinted 1990.

Grollman, E. *Talking About Death: A Dialogue Between Parents and Children, 3rd Edition*. Beacon Press, 1991.

Hamley, D. *Tigger and Friends*. William Morrow & Co., 1989. O.P.

Heegaard, Marge Eaton. *Coping With Death and Grief*. Lerner Publications Company, 1990.

_____. *When Someone Very Special Dies: Children Can Learn to Cope With Grief.* Woodland Press, 1988.

_____. *Saying Good-bye to Your Pet: Children Can Learn to Cope With Grief.* Fairview Press, _____, 2001.

Hewett, J. *Rosalie*. William Morrow & Co., 1987. O.P.

Holmes, E.T. *Amy's Goose*. HarperCollins, 1977. Reissued 1992.

Jewett, C.L. *Helping Children Cope with Separation and Loss*. The Harvard Common Press, 1994. Revised edition.

Mellonie, B. *Lifetimes: The Beautiful Way to Explain Death to Children*. Bantam Doubleday Dell Publishing, 1987.

Morehead, D. *A Special Place for Charlee: A Child's Companion Through Pet Loss*. Partners in Publishing, LLC. 1996.

Rogers, F. *When A Pet Dies*. Paper Star, 1988. Reissued 1998.

Rylant, C. *Dog Heaven*. Scholastic, 1995.

_____. *Cat Heaven*. Scholastic, 1997.

Sanford, D. *It Must Hurt a Lot: A Child's Book About Death*. Multnomah Press, 1985.

Sibbitt, S. *Oh Where Has My Pet Gone? A Pet Loss Memory Book, Ages 3-10*. B. Libby Press, 1991. O.P.

Stein, S.B. *About Dying: An Open Family Book for Parents and Children Together*. Walker & Company, 1983.

Tousley, M. *Children and Pet Loss: A Guide for Helping*. Our Pals, 1996.

Viorst, J. *The Tenth Good Thing About Barney*. Econo-Clad Books, 1999.

Warren, P. *Where Love Goes*. Art After Five, 1992.

White, E.B. *Charlotte's Web*. HarperCollins, 1952. Reprint 1999.

Wilhelm, H. *I'll Always Love You*. Random House, 1990.

Wolfelt, A. *Helping Children Cope with Grief.* Accelerated Development, 1983.

Wright, B.R. *The Cat Next Door*. Holiday House Books, 1991.

Pet Loss

Anderson, M. *Coping with Sorrow on the Loss of Your Pet.* Second Edition, Alpine Publications, 1996.

Antinori, D. *Journey Through Pet Loss, Revised Edition.* Yoko Spirit Publications, 2000. Audiotape.

Barton-Ross, Cheri, and Baron-Sorensen, Jane. *Pet Loss and Human Emotion*, Taylor & Francis Group, 1998.

Church, J.A. *Joy in a Woolly Coat: Living With, Loving, and Letting Go of Treasured Animal Friends.* H.J. Kramer, Inc., 1988.

Harris, E. *Pet Loss: A Spiritual Guide*. Llewellyn Publications, 1997.

Hunt, Laurel E, Editor. *Angel Pawprints: Reflections on Loving and Losing a Canine Companion*. Hyperion, 2000.

Ironside, V. *Good-bye, Dear Friend: Coming to Terms With the Death of a Pet*. Robson Book Ltd., 1997.

Kay, W.J. et. al., eds, *Pet Loss and Human Bereavement*. Iowa State University Press, 1988.

_____. *Euthanasia of the Companion Animal: The Impact on Pet Owners, Veterinarians and Society.* The Charles Press, 1988.

Kosins, M.C. *Maya's First Rose: Diary of a Very Special Love*. Willard Books, 1992.

Kowalski, G. *Good-bye Friend: Healing Wisdom for Anyone Who Has Ever Lost a Pet.* Stillpoint Publishing, 1997.

Kowalski, G., Regan, T., and Wolfe, A. *The Souls of Animals.* Second Edition, Stillpoint Publishing, 1999.

Kurz, G. *Cold Noses at the Pearly Gates.* Gary Kurz, 1997.

Lagoni, L., Butler, C., and Hetts, S. *The Human-Animal Bond and Grief.* W.B. Saunders Publishing, 1994

_____. *Friends for Life: Loving and Losing Your Animal Companion.* Sounds True Audio, 1997. Audiotape.

Lemieux, C. *Coping With the Loss of a Pet*, Revised Edition. Wallace R. Clark Co., 1989.

Mooney, S. *A Snowflake in My Hand.* Lightning Source, 1983. Reissued 1995.

Nieberg, H.A. and Fisher, A. *Pet Loss: A Thoughtful Guide for Adults and Children.* Harperperennial Library, 1982. Reprint Edition 1996.

Peterson, L. *Surviving the Heartbreak of Choosing Death for Your Pet: Your Personal Guide for Dealing with Pet Euthanasia.* Greentree Publishing, 1997.

Quackenbush, J., and Graveline, D. *When Your Pet Dies: How to Cope With Your Feelings.* Pocket Books, 1988.

Quackenbush, J. and Voith, V., eds. *Symposium on the Human-Companion Animal Bond.* W. B. Saunders Company, March 1985.

Quintana, M., Veleba, S., and King, H. *It's Okay to Cry.* K& K Communications, 2000.

Sife, W. *The Loss of a Pet.* Revised and expanded edition. Hungry Minds, Inc., 1998.

Smith, K., ed. *Healing the Pain of Pet Loss: Letters in Memoriam.* The Charles Press, 1997.

Steinbach, D. *Loving, Caring, Letting Go Without Guilt: A Compassionate But Straightforward Look at Pet Euthanasia.* Willow Bend Publishing, 1997.

Stern, M., and Cropper, S. *Loving and Losing a Pet: A Psychologist and a Veterinarian Share Their Wisdom.* Jason Aronson, 1998.

Stockton, Anne. *Honey-bun: An Enchanting Memoir About an Exceptional Cat.* Educare Press, 1999.

Sussman, M., ed. *Pets and the Family.* The Haworth Press, Inc., 1985.

Tousley, M., and Heuerman, K. *The Final Farewell: Preparing for and Mourning the Loss of Your Pet.* Our Pals, 1997.

Wagner, T.L. *Legacies of Love: A Gentle Guide to Healing From the Loss of Your Animal Loved One.* Matter of the Heart, 1998. Audiotape.

Give the Gift of Healing and Love
to Your Friends and Loved Ones

Order Form

Please send me ____ copies of *Maltese Crossing* at $19.95 each, plus $3.00 shipping for the first book and $2.00 for each additional book.

Name_____

Company_____

Address_____

City_____ State_____ Zip Code_____

How May We Reach You?

Telephone_____ Fax _____

E-mail_____

A check or money order enclosed.

Please make your check payable to:

Golden Reflections Publications
601C Sixteenth Street #215
Golden, Colorado 80401

You may also E-mail your order to: drpd@mac.com

Give the Gift of Healing and Love
to Your Friends and Loved Ones

Order Form

Please send me ____ copies of *Maltese Crossing* at $19.95 each, plus $3.00 shipping for the first book and $2.00 for each additional book.

Name_____

Company_____

Address_____

City_____ State_____ Zip Code_____

How May We Reach You?

Telephone_____ Fax _____

E-mail_____

A check or money order enclosed.

Please make your check payable to:

Golden Reflections Publications
601C Sixteenth Street #215
Golden, Colorado 80401

You may also E-mail your order to: drpd@mac.com